DICK HAMILTON'S FOOTBALL TEAM

OR

A YOUNG MILLIONAIRE ON THE GRIDIRON

HOWARD R. GARIS

[ZHINGOORA BOOKS]

This edition is published by
Zhingoora Books.

Apart from any fair dealing for the purposes of research or private study, or criti-cism or review, this publication may only be reproduced, stored or transmitted, in any form or by any means, with the prior permission in writing of the publishers. All disputes are subject to exclusive jurisdiction of Mandsaur Courts only. For any suggestions and feedback or book on new concept/domain, please contact us at the email given below.

contact@Zhingoora.com

PREFACE

My Dear Boys:

In writing this, the fourth volume of the "Dick Hamilton Series," telling of the doings of the young millionaire on the gridiron, I have had one particular thought in mind. That was to make as interesting a story as possible for you. Now that it is finished, it is for you to say whether or not you like it. I trust I may be pardoned if I say I hope that you will.

When Dick returned to the Kentfield Military Academy after his vacation on his steam yacht, he found the football team of which he was a member, in poor shape. In fact the eleven was laughed at by other military schools, one of which refused to accept a challenge that Kentfield sent.

How Dick hired a coach from Princeton and one from Yale, and how they "whipped" the team into shape, how championship material was made from them, you will find told of in this book.

There is also related how Dick worked to save his father's wealth by getting possession of certain electric road stock, which was held by a crabbed old man who disliked cadets and football. Of course there is also something about the bulldog, Grit, in this book, and about Uncle Ezra Larabee, and the doings of our hero's friends and enemies are fully set forth.

Again expressing the hope that you will find this story interesting, and that you will care to hear more of Dick Hamilton, I remain,

Yours cordially,

Howard R. Garis.

CONTENTS

CHAPTER

CHAPTER I

TURNED DOWN

"Well, if those fellows haven't got nerve!"

"I should say so! Why it's a direct insult!"

"We ought to challenge 'em to a sham battle. I know we could put it all over 'em at that game, if we can't at football; eh, fellows?"

"Sure thing!" came in a chorus from a group of cadets who surrounded a rather fat, good-natured companion. The latter held an open letter in his hand, and had just finished reading it, the contents causing the various exclamations.

"Say, Beeby," spoke Paul Drew, "are you sure it isn't a joke? Maybe they're just trying to have fun with us."

"Fun! This is serious enough," replied the stout youth, "Frank Anderson, manager of the Blue Hill Academy eleven, takes pains to be very explicit. Listen."

Once more Beeby read the note.

"In reply to your challenge for a series of football games, in the Military League, and your request that we give you a contest at an early date, we regret to say that our team cannot play yours. To be frank, we do not think that your eleven is in the same class with ours. We won nearly every game we played last season, and, you know, as well as do we, that Kentfield was away down at the tail end.

"It is the sense of the Athletic Committee of Blue Hill Military Academy that we must play with teams of greater strength and in a better class than the one that represents Kentfield. If you wish, perhaps I can arrange some games with our second team, but not with the first.

"Regretting very much that we cannot accept your challenge, I remain,

"Yours very truly,

"Frank Anderson, Manager."

"Well, wouldn't that put a crimp in your bayonet?" demanded John Stiver.

"They'll condescend to let their second team come over and beat us!" exclaimed Ray Dutton sarcastically. "Bur-r-r-r!"

"Oh, say, this makes me mad!" spluttered Beeby, and he made as though to tear the letter to shreds.

"Don't! Wait a minute!" begged Paul Drew. "Let's talk this over a bit, first. Something's got to be done about it. We can't let this insult pass. I wish Dick Hamilton was here."

"Where is he?" asked Beeby, as he folded the crumpled letter.

"He went to town to send a message home, I guess. He'll soon be back."

"Let's go to the Sacred Pig, and talk this over," suggested Dutton, as he opened a few buttons on his tightly fitting parade coat, for drill among the cadets was just over, and they had not yet gotten into their fatigue uniforms.

"Yes, let's plan some scheme to get even with those Blue Hill snobs," added Paul. "Say Toots," he went on to one of the janitors about the academy, "if you see Mr. Hamilton, just send him over to the Sacred Pig, will you?"

"I sure will, Mr. Drew," and Toots, so called because he was generally whistling some military air, saluted.

The cadets still talking among themselves about the churlish letter they had received, passed on toward a society chapter house—that of the Sacred Pig—one of the most exclusive organizations among the cadets of Kentfield.

"If Anderson wanted to turn us down why didn't he simply say that all their dates were filled?" demanded Beeby, on whom the blow fell especially heavy, as he was manager of the eleven.

"Well, if the truth *had* to be told I suppose it might as well come out first as last," spoke Paul frankly.

"The truth!" demanded Innis Beeby, half indignantly.

"Yes! Kentfield hasn't a good team, and we all know it. It's no one's fault in particular," went on Paul, "but we don't practice enough, we don't play well enough together, and we were the tail-enders last year. We might as well face the music."

"Even if it isn't particularly harmonious," commented Innis bitterly, as he walked up the steps of the handsome society house. "Well, let's see what we can do."

The rest of the cadets followed, to be greeted by a number of other students who were already gathered in the pleasant reading room. There was a general movement toward the newcomers when the news quickly flashed around, and the letter was passed from hand to hand.

There were more comments, caustic ones in the main, and had Manager Anderson been present he would probably have had several challenges to fight, for the feeling was bitter against him.

"You can't beat this for nerve!" declared Jim Watkins.

"I say, let's get up a good team, and force 'em to play us," suggested Teddy Naylor.

"How are you going to force 'em?" demanded Frank Rutley.

"Why, play such fast and snappy games that they can't refuse us—get in the champion class—*make* 'em recognize us."

"Oh, it's easy enough to talk," murmured Innis, "but when it comes to a football team——"

"What's the matter with the football team?" demanded a new voice, and a tall, good-looking cadet, bronzed almost to a copper color, came in. "Are we going to have practice to-day?"

"Hello, Dick!"

"Glad you came in, Hamilton."

"You're just in time to hear the news."

These were some of the expressions that greeted the advent of the newcomer. Dick Hamilton pressed up into the group of indignant lads, and accepted the letter which Innis held out to him.

"Read that!" spluttered the stout lad.

As Dick read a dull flush crept up under his coat of tan.

"Um!" was his only comment for a moment. Then he said: "Well, he didn't soften it any. But how about it; isn't it almost true?"

"That's what I say," cried Paul Drew.

"We haven't a very good team, that's a fact," admitted Jim Watkins, who played centre.

"Oh, bosh! You fellows make me tired," declared Innis. "You are almost as bad as Anderson."

"Well, we ought to perk up."

"Oh pshaw! We can play all right."

"All we need is practice."

"And a little harder work against the scrub."

These and other comments flew back and forth. Dick Hamilton strolled toward an easy chair near a table. Casually he picked up a paper, and glanced over it as the discussion waxed warmer. There were two sides, one set of cadets holding that the eleven was not so bad, and the others maintaining that the players should not shut their eyes to facts, but endeavor to correct their faults. Both factions numbered members of the team, so it could not be said that prejudice shaped the opinions.

"Well, what do think about it, Dick?" asked Paul at length, as he sat down beside his roommate.

"About what?" asked the young millionaire, somewhat absently-mindedly.

"Well, for the love of mustard! Have you been dreaming while all this racket was going on? And you read that letter, too! I say, Dick, what's up?"

"Oh, yes, I remember now. I was thinking of something else," and Dick recovered himself with an effort, seeming to bring his thoughts back from some distant point. "The football team."

"Of course, the eleven—or, rather, the woeful lack of one. What's to be done, Dick? I rather thought you might have a scheme, when you heard the news."

There was silence in the room for a moment, and nearly all eyes were turned on Dick Hamilton.

"A plan—yes—I might—by Jove, fellows, I believe I have a plan!" he exclaimed suddenly. "It ought to work, too. We've got to have the best team on the gridiron in the Military League, and just now I thought of something that will bring it about."

"Then in the name of the two-horned rhinoceros speak it quickly!" begged Innis. "Say something so I can get back at this dub Anderson. I'll write him a hot one!"

"Oh, it will take a little while to put it through," went on the young millionaire, "but I believe I can do it. Now my plan is——"

At that moment one of the pages employed at the society house, which was sort of cadet club, approached the eager group of students.

"Beg pardon," the page said, "but here is a telegram that just came for Mr. Hamilton."

Dick tore open the yellow envelope. He read the message at a glance and seemed to start as at the receipt of unwelcome news.

"I've got to go out for a while," he said to his chums. "I'll be back as soon as possible. This is important."

"But your football plan," begged Innis.

"I'll tell it when I come back," called Dick Hamilton as he hurried out, leaving a much-wondering group of cadets looking after him.

CHAPTER II

WAR ON MR. HAMILTON

"The rumor is true then," mused Dick, as he hurried out of the chapter house, and started toward the telegraph office. "I rather hoped it would prove to be *only* a rumor, but if dad has heard it also, there must be something in it. Now I wonder if I can get hold of any more news, so I can wire him? Let's see, what is it he says."

Dick glanced again at the telegram that had been brought to him. It was from his father, Mortimer Hamilton, a multi-millionaire, and was in answer to a message the youth had sent his parent that day.

"Have heard rumor you speak of," the father's message read, "see if you can learn more. Wire me at once. Our trolley interests are threatened. They are trying to get me out of control."

"If they do that it will be a hard blow for dad," said Dick, as he hurried along.

Of late Mr. Hamilton had put much money in an important trolley line, and had called in several other investments so that he might buy more of the stock. A large part of his fortune was now involved in the electric road, and if he lost the controlling interest it might mean his ruin.

Consequently our hero was not a little alarmed. Only that day he had heard the disquieting rumor. It came from a fellow cadet, Sam Porter, whose father was very wealthy. In the hearing of Dick, Sam had accidently mentioned a deal his father was putting through, involving the very electric line in which Mr. Hamilton was so vitally interested. But then Sam did not know how much of the stock Mr. Hamilton owned, in fact he did not know that Dick's parent was at all interested.

But the young millionaire—for Dick was that in his own right—had taken alarm at once, and had immediately wired his father.

"And now I must see if I can get any further information," mused the lad. "It will hardly be safe to ask Porter directly. I wonder if I could pump him through Jake Weston, his crony? I'll try it, after I wire dad that I'm on the job."

While Dick is on his way to send the message I will take the opportunity to explain to you something more about him, and also something about the previous books in this series. As I told you in the first volume, entitled "Dick Hamilton's Fortune," he was left a large sum by his mother, who had been dead some years. But he must comply with certain conditions of Mrs. Hamilton's will, before he could get control of his millions.

One stipulation was that he must use his funds to make some sort of a paying investment. If he failed in this he would have to spend some time with a crabbed old uncle, Mr. Ezra Larabee, who lived in a gloomy place called Dankville.

Dick tried several schemes to make money for himself, but, as may be imagined from a lad who had had no experience, one plan after another failed. But, at the last moment a small investment he had made, to help a poor, but fine-charactered lad, named Henry Darby, start in the junk and iron business, proved wonderfully successful, and Dick fulfilled the conditions of the will. Uncle Ezra was much provoked that he was not to get control of his dead sister's son, and his millions, but he was routed, and had to flee from Grit, the prize bulldog Dick owned.

"Dick Hamilton's Cadet Days," was the title of the second volume. In that I told how Dick, to further comply with the instructions in his mother's will, went to the Kentfield Military Academy. There he was to make his way, unaided by any influence of his millions.

He had an up-hill struggle, for there was a prejudice against him. But he was delighted with the military life. He took part in the drills, in the cavalry exercises, he helped to win a victory in a big sham battle, and he fought a duel that had a curious outcome. He was wounded in a broad sword combat, and was the means of saving the life of his enemy Dutton, who later became his friend.

Kentfield Academy was located in one of the middle western states, near Lake Wagatook. Colonel James Masterly was superintendent, Major Henry Rockford, commandant, and Major Franklin Webster, of the United States Army, was the instructor in military tactics. Captain Hayden was head master, Captain Grantly in charge of the science classes, and Captain Nelton of those in mathematics.

Dick, while attending there, was the means of solving the mystery of the identity of "Toots," the whistling janitor, and when the society house of the Sacred Pig burned down, and it was found that the insurance had expired, Dick rebuilt the meeting place in much handsomer style than formerly, thereby gaining the everlasting admiration of the cadets.

Dick and his chums had many social pleasures, and if you care to know how well they could dance, Miss Nellie Fordice, Mabel Hanford, Nettie French or Mildred Adams could tell you.

Dick spent his first summer's vacation at Hamilton Corners, a town named after his father, who was the principal citizen there, as well as owner of many local enterprises, including a bank. In the fall Dick returned to the academy, and was promoted to a captaincy.

In the third volume of the series, entitled "Dick Hamilton's Steam Yacht," I told of a long trip our hero took in a steam yacht which he purchased from his ample fortune. With a party of friends he went to Cuba.

Uncle Ezra Larabee thought that Dick did very wrong to spend so much money, so the crabbed old man conceived a plan of kidnapping the youth, and taking him in charge, to "teach him frugal ways," as he said.

Mr. Larabee hired a small steamer, and set off after his nephew. He did kidnap a youth—or, rather the men he hired did—but it was not Dick, and that made all the confusion. However, Dick had trouble enough, for his yacht was stolen, and he was left marooned with his friends on a lonely island. How they built a raft, set out to sea, how they were rescued, and the pursuit after Dick's yacht, aboard which was his mean uncle—all this you will find set down in the book.

After his trip Dick came back up north. All too soon the academy opened, and our hero had to dock his fine vessel, don his uniform, and get back to his studies. But he did not mind, once he was among his classmates again, and he had been "buckling down to hard work" as he expressed it, for a few weeks, when the events narrated in the first chapter took place.

Dick's interest was divided between anxiety over the plight that might befall his father, and the "slump" that hung over the football eleven.

"I hope my football scheme works," he said. "But I can't think about that now. I must help out dad. It's too bad, after all the work he put in on getting that trolley line in shape, to be threatened with the loss of it. I must do all I can to stop it. I'll just wire him that I'll be on the lookout, and then I'll see what I can pick up from Porter or Weston."

Dick knew where to find the two cadets in question. They were first-year students, and were not members of the Sacred Pig, though they would have given much to join. Dick was not especially friendly with them, but he now resolved to cultivate their acquaintance, at least long enough to see if he could get on the track of the men who were seeking to wrest the control of the trolley line from Mr. Hamilton.

After sending his second message, Dick strolled toward a "fashionable" pool club in town, where many of the more "sporty" cadets spent much of their time, when not at study.

"Hello, Hamilton!" greeted Porter. "Have a cue. I'm tired of playing Weston. He's too easy."

Dick was a good pool and billiard player, and had two fine tables at home. But somehow he did not play well on this occasion. Porter easily beat him.

"I'll try again," said the young millionaire, and when the second game was well under way he gradually led the talk around to business matters.

"My dad is great on business, and deals," chuckled Porter as he made a good shot, and finished up with a run of six. "He's got a deal on now that will put a few crimps in a couple of people that think themselves some pumpkins."

"Yes?" queried Dick, as he missed what seemed to be an easy shot.

"Sure. That trolley deal I mentioned. But I forgot, I'm not supposed to talk about it. Only there's some gazabo of a millionaire, down east or somewhere, that will get the gaff all right. Say, I hear your dad is pretty well up in business, Ham?"

"Yes, he has a number of interests," spoke Dick, as he chalked his cue for a billiard game. He was hoping it would not develope that he was the son of the "gazabo" in question.

"Well, my dad is the limit," went on Porter. "When this trolley deal goes through, as it will, he'll be several millions better off. It's war to the knife, so he told me. I don't know who he's fighting, but it's some one."

Dick knew, but he kept still.

"It sure is war," he reflected as he made ready to shoot. "I must learn all I can about the plans of Porter's father, and the men who are in with him. Then I can help dad. And then—there's the football trouble. Well, Dick Hamilton," and he paused for a serious moment before making a nice shot that required plenty of "English" on it, "you sure have your hands full."

CHAPTER III

DICK'S PLAN

Rain was coming down heavily when Dick finished the game, and he looked out from the poolroom with rather a rueful face as he heard the downpour.

"I'll run you back in my car," offered Porter. "We can stop at Martin's on the way in, and have a jolly little supper. What do you say, Ham?"

Dick rather resented being called "Ham" by a youth who had known him but a short time. Likewise he did not care to stop at Martin's. So he covered his dislike as best he could, and answered:

"No, thank you. I have some business to attend to, and I don't want to keep you. Go on back to Kentfield, and I'll take a taxicab when I've finished with my matters."

"Oh, I suppose you follow in the footsteps of the governor, and are in business too," almost sneered Weston.

"Well, I help my father whenever I can," answered Dick, as the blood surged up under his coat of tan. "Sorry I couldn't beat you, Mr. Porter. I hope to have better luck next time."

"You want to bring along all the luck you have, Hamilton," declared the rich lad, as he put on his coat, while Dick settled for the games, which he had almost purposely lost in order that he might have a better excuse for talking to Porter. "I'm a pretty good shot," and he laughed in Dick's face.

"So I see," agreed Dick.

"Then you won't motor back with us?" asked Porter, for he had an expensive machine, which was in the repair shop a good part of the time, owing to his reckless driving.

"No, I've got several matters to attend to," answered Dick, and he watched the two cronies going out together.

The storm continued, the rain coming down harder than ever, and, as Dick had no umbrella he decided to go down to the telegraph office in a taxicab, a service but newly installed in the college town, but which was taken advantage of by many students.

Dick was not a spendthrift, and he knew the value of money. Still, when he did not have to count his dollars, he did not see the harm in spending a few in hiring an auto cab, when he had no umbrella.

A few minutes later he was bowling along the rain-swept streets toward the telegraph office which he had but recently left.

"Dad will think I'm making the wires hot," he mused, as the taxicab careened along, "but I guess I'd better keep him informed right up to date. That Mr. Porter means business, if I'm any judge. Probably he has a syndicate of rich men back of him, and they are trying to get control of father's interests. But we'll put a stop to that if possible.

"What a cad that Porter fellow is, with his billiard shots, and his cigarettes! I could have beaten him easily, if I'd wanted to, but if I had he might have turned sulky, and wouldn't have talked so much. As it is I've gotten some good information out of him."

Dick leaned back on the cushions and let his thoughts wander free. As he had said, there were two big problems ahead of him. He wanted to see the cadet football team triumph on the gridiron, and he wanted to help his father get ahead of his enemies.

Both matters were important to Dick, for he realized that his father's interests, being now so much bound up in the trolley line, would suffer seriously if antagonists got in control.

As for football, our hero, who was one of the best members of the team, wanted to see his eleven at the head of the Military League.

And, for several seasons past Kentfield had been the tail-ender, and practically out of the league. True, they had won some games, and big ones, too, but it was more like a sudden spurt, and then the cadets seemed to go "stale," and played in such poor form that inferior teams beat them.

"It's got to stop," said Dick to himself. "We've got to win, and if I can put my plan through, and I don't see why I can't, we'll be at the top of the heap pretty soon. That is if the fellows will work. And they've got to! By Jove I'm not going to stay at a college where a little dinky team like the one from Blue Hill, can put it all over us, and write such letters as Beeby got to-day.

"Poor Beeby! He felt it a heap. It was like the time when we were marooned on that island, and he managed to snap-shot a lot of birds, and came in to tell us about them. We thought he meant he had killed them for dinner. Oh, that was a time all right!"

and Dick fell to thinking of the adventures he had gone through when he was taking the first voyage in his steam yacht.

The taxicab came to a sudden stop. The young millionaire looked out, and through the rain he saw the telegraph office.

"I guess the man will think I'm running a regular brokerage business," he reflected as he alighted and went in. He sent a message to his father, telling what he had heard from Porter during the billiard game, and warning Mr. Hamilton to be on the watch for treachery.

"There, I guess that will make dad get busy," said the lad. "Now I'll wait for further instructions, and devote a little time to planning out what I want to do for the football team. We've got to be champions of the league or I'll know the reason why. What's the good of money if it can't get you what you want?"

"Where to now, sir?" asked the taxi-driver, as Dick got in the machine again. "Like to go around town for a while? Most of the cadets do when they get out."

"Back to the college," ordered Dick a bit curtly, for he did not like the familiar tone of the man.

"Hum, he must be one of those tight-wads," thought the driver, as he threw in his gears and started off. "I like a fellow that spends money."

If he had known how much Dick Hamilton *could* have spent had our hero been so inclined, the taxi-man might have had a different opinion of him.

The machine was bowling along at a good speed, through the principal street of the town, preparatory to turning off on the road that led to the military academy. It was a cab with the front of glass, and Dick could look out at one side of the driver, and observe what was going on.

Suddenly, as they crossed a side street, an elderly man, with a big, old-fashioned umbrella held low over his head, ran out directly in front of the cab.

"Look out! Stop!" cried Dick, involuntarily jumping up. "You'll run him down!"

The driver was on the alert, however, and jammed on the brakes with a practiced hand, and a quick foot. With a shudder of springs and a shriek of metal the cab came to a stop. Not before, however, it had run into the man with the big umbrella, upsetting him, though so gently that he was not hurt. His rain-shield however, was crumpled up and his legs were entangled in it.

Before the driver could leave his seat, Dick had jumped out and gone to the aid of the pedestrian.

"I hope you're not hurt!" the lad exclaimed, as he helped the aged man to arise. "I'm very sorry it happened. I guess you held your umbrella so low that you couldn't see us coming."

For clearly it was not the fault of the driver that the accident had occurred.

"Ha! Hum! So that's what you think, eh?" demanded the man in a rasping voice, as he fairly grabbed the broken umbrella from Dick's hand. "Here I be, walking peaceably along the street, trying to protect myself from the rain, when you reckless military students come along in one of those fire-snorting new-fangled automobiles, and run me down. It was all your fault, and if I could see a policeman I'd have you both locked up! How many of those tin soldiers from the military academy have you in there anyhow? Cadets! Humph! Much better be at some honest business instead of learning to kill folks! Are there any more of you? If there are, come out, and I'll give you a piece of my mind! Learning murder as a fine art! How many in there?" and he glared at the taxicab.

"I'm the only one," said Dick modestly.

"Hum! Too mean to let some one else ride with you, I reckon. Well, it was all your fault, and you'll have to settle with me. Duncaster is my name, Enos Duncaster, and I don't intend to be imposed upon."

Dick could not help thinking how like his uncle Erza Mr. Duncaster was.

"It was your fault, you old hayseeder!" cried the taxicab man with a nervous voice, for he had been mortally afraid of a fatal accident. "What do you want to run under a machine that way for? Hey? Why can't you look where you're going?"

"Young man!" exclaimed Mr. Duncaster in a calm voice, "if I didn't know that you were excited you'd pay dearly for this. You don't know me, but I'll say, for your information, that I own enough stock in this taxicab company to have you discharged. I'm sorry I ever invested in it, but I didn't know them machines were so rip-snorting. Now you can go on, but first give me your names."

"What for?" demanded the driver suspiciously.

"Oh, in case I find I have worse injuries than a broken umbrella," replied the elderly man with a half-smile. "I may want to bring suit against the company in which I hold stock."

"Well, my name is Martin," replied the driver, "James Martin. I certainly didn't mean to run you down, Mr. Duncaster. But the rain was in my eyes, and——"

"That will do," said the man with an air of authority. "Now who are you—my young soldier lad? I don't believe in this war business, but the country seems to be going crazy over it, so I might as well keep still. Who are you?"

"Hamilton—Dick Hamilton is my name."

"Hum—Hamilton—no relation to Mortimer Hamilton; are you?"

"He is my father."

"What."

"I say he is my father."

"Why that's odd—I'm—no, never mind—so you're Mortimer Hamilton's son; eh? I heard he had one, and that he was going to some sort of military school. I'm sorry to see it. And so you're the one who ran me down? And you haven't a crowd of roistering students with you?"

"No, I'm all alone. I've been attending to some business for my father."

"Hum! Business, yes. That's about all Mortimer Hamilton does. Well, you may go. I know where to find both of you in case I want you."

The odd old man gathered up what was left of his umbrella, and, declining the aid of a policeman who came up to see what the gathering crowd meant, Mr. Duncaster walked off.

"We got out of that lucky," commented the taxi-driver, as Dick re-entered the vehicle. "I sure thought he would fire me. Who'd think old man Duncaster would be up here?"

"Is he really a wealthy man?" asked Dick.

"You bet he is. He lives away down in the country somewhere, and all he does is to cut off the interest coupons from his bonds. He's a millionaire, but you'd never think it to look at him. The idea of walking, when he could hire a machine and ride. But he's close—awful close."

"I hope he doesn't make trouble," commented our hero. "If he does, let me know. In spite of who he is I think it was his own fault that we hit him."

"Sure it was," declared the driver heartily.

Dick was soon back at school and his first visit was to the society house of the Sacred Pig. He found only a few of his cadet chums there, as it was nearing mess time, and they had gone to dress for the meal.

"Well, you're a fine fellow to run off and desert us the way you did!" cried Innis Beeby, as he clapped Dick on the shoulder. "What's your great scheme about a football team? The fellows are half wild trying to guess. Couldn't you explain before you hiked away?"

"No, didn't have time."

"Then tell me now."

"No, I'd like all the fellows to be together when they hear it and then they won't get it twisted. I'll meet you all here after grub, and tell you what I think of doing."

"All right; it's a go."

Dick found a goodly crowd waiting for him in the main room of the club house, for word had gone around of what was about to take place. Our hero wasted no time on preliminaries.

"Boys," he began, "you know as well as I do, that we have received an insulting letter from the Blue Hill academy. Our football team, of which I have the honor to be a member——"

"Hurray for the team!" cried Paul Drew. "Long may she wave, o'er the land——"

"Order in the ranks!" cried Innis Beeby, who was presiding.

"Our team needs strengthening," went on Dick. "There is no use ignoring the facts before us. We never have had a first class team—that is, to judge by the records of the past. We have not a good team now, and I'm as bad as the worst member, so I'm not shielding myself. That being the case, what's to be done?"

"Get a new team!" called someone.

"Revamp the old one," cried another.

"That's my idea exactly," went on Dick. "We must use the material we have, but with this restriction—there must be a fair field and no favors. The best men must be picked on the team."

"Sure!" cried someone.

"But who's going to do the picking?" demanded Beeby.

"That's what I'm coming to," went on Dick. "I was going to tell you my plan, when I had to leave this afternoon."

"Tell it now!" was the general shout.

"This is it!" replied the young millionaire. "You know what good coaching can do for a team. I think that's what we need, and it is casting no reflection on the present coaches, for we all know they can devote only a little time to the work. Now what I propose is this: We can get two of the best coaches in the country—say one from Yale and one from Princeton. They can come here, and in a few weeks I'm sure they can whip our team into shape. We have the material—all it needs is to be developed."

"That's right—but how can we afford to pay for a Yale and a Princeton coach?" demanded George Hall.

"I'll attend to that end," replied Dick calmly. "This is my treat. I want Kentfield to have the best eleven in the league, and if coaching can do it we'll have it. Then we can win some games. I'll pay for the coaches, and we'll see what they can do. That was my football scheme. What do you think of it, fellows?"

CHAPTER IV

FOOTBALL PRACTICE

For a few seconds no one spoke after Dick Hamilton had mentioned his plan for improving the Kentfield eleven. But at length, with a long-drawn sigh of satisfaction, Innis remarked:

"Dick; you're a trump!—a brick!—an ice-cream brick on a hot day!—you're all to the mustard!—a——"

"Cut it out!" cried our hero, "can't you see how I'm blushing? But seriously, fellows, is my plan all right?"

"I should say it was!" exclaimed Paul Drew.

"But look at what it's going to cost," objected George Hall. "Those Yale and Princeton coaches are high-fliers—that is, if you can get them to come—and then besides their salary, we'll have to board 'em. Though I s'pose we could put 'em up at the Pig, provided they won't scrap all the while over different training plans."

"Oh, I fancy that part will be all right," remarked Teddy Naylor.

"But do you think you can get any Yale or Princeton coaches to come here—to Kentfield—with her poor, old, broken-down team—that is according to Anderson," spoke Frank Rutley.

"Well, of course we'll have to take a chance on that," replied Dick. "If we can't get men from those two colleges we can try some others. But dad is an old Princeton grad. and I have sort of a distant forty-second cousin who was once a star half-back at Yale. I might get them to put in a good word for us."

"Hurray!" cried Innis in the excitement and exuberance of the moment. "That's the stuff! Now we'll wipe up the ground with those Blue Hill snobs! Whoop-la!"

He shot out a sturdy fist, and squarely hit a football that Teddy Naylor was balancing on his hand. The spheroid flew straight and true across the room, and caught John Stiver on the chin. Stiver at that moment happened to be looking at the sporting page of a paper and did not see the ball coming. Consequently it was quite a surprise, and he went over backward against Paul Drew, both going down in a heap.

"I say, who did that?" cried John, as he arose with the symptoms of wrath in his eyes.

"I did, old chap!" confessed Innis contritely. "You see I felt so good I wanted to start something. I beg your pardon."

"Granted. But you certainly started something all right," remarked John grimly. "There goes Drew's nose bleeding. You sure started something all right."

"Oh, I don't mind," responded Dick's roommate, as he went to a toilet room to staunch the flow of blood. "If we get a good team and play some stiff games I'll probably have worse than this before the season is over."

Innis went out with Paul to assist in attending to the bleeding member, and the others resumed their football talk. There was but one opinion about Dick's plan—everybody said it was just what was needed, and to all suggestions that it would cost a mint of money, the young millionaire declared that it would be worth all it cost him.

"What's the use of having a fortune if you don't spend it?" he asked with a smile. "Though I suppose if my Uncle Ezra hears about my latest scheme he'll try again to kidnap me, to stop me from carrying it out. But he isn't here, is he Grit, old boy?" and Dick stooped over to pet his bulldog, who crouched at his feet, the animal being an honorary member of the Sacred Pig Society.

Grit growled at the mention of the name of Uncle Ezra. He had a deep antipathy to that gentleman, and with reason, for Mr. Larabee hated dogs, and kicked Grit on the sly every time he got the chance.

"Then it's all settled," remarked Dick, when Paul and Innis had come back to the general room. "I'll get busy writing some letters, and we'll see what we can do. It's lucky the season hasn't started yet, for we have plenty of time to get into shape."

"Yes, and we'll not only do up Blue Hill good and brown, but we'll put it all over Mooretown and some of the other teams in the Military League," declared Innis. "But you fellows must get at practice, and try and harden yourselves. I wish Bert Cameron was here—I don't know how he's going to take to this new coaching idea."

"Oh, Bert won't mind," declared Jim Watkins. "He'll be only too glad to be relieved of the coaching, for I heard him say he was trying for an extra exam. in maths, and he needs all the time he can get."

Bert, who was a star football player, had given up active participation in the game to act as coach for Kentfield. But, as his chums well knew, he had not the necessary time to devote to the work of telling them what to do and how to do it, and the team suffered in consequence.

However, the mention of this gave Dick an idea. He did not want to hurt the feelings of Bert, and, when the coach entered the club a little later the matter was mentioned to him.

"Go ahead, grand idea," he declared and his enthusiasm was not forced. "I know I haven't been keeping you fellows up to the mark, and I'll be glad to see some one here who can. Besides, I need all the time I can get to bone away at my maths."

"Then I'll go ahead," declared the young millionaire. "I'll have the new coaches here in a week if I can get them, and I'll meet any financial demand they make."

"That's the way to talk!" cried Paul, clapping his chum on the back with such energy that Dick uttered a protest.

When our hero turned in at taps that night, his mind was filled with two main thoughts. One was the future of the football team, and the other was the trouble that threatened his father. Then another remembrance came to him.

"I wonder who that Mr. Duncaster is that we so nearly ran over?" mused Dick. "He must know dad. He's a queer sort of a character, I guess."

Dick little thought of what an important part in the future of himself and his father this same Mr. Duncaster was to play.

"Well, I'll see if I can get any more information from Porter about the deal his father is in," said Dick to himself, as he turned over to compose himself for sleep. "There must be more than one man in the game, and it's up to me to find out who the others are, so dad can be on his guard. I hope he doesn't lose control of the trolley, for a lot of small investors have put all their money in it, and if other interested men get hold of it the investors might lose all they have. I guess that's why dad is so worried. I'll cultivate the acquaintance of Porter and Weston, though I don't care much for them."

A better day for football practice could not have been desired. There was just enough crispness in the air, and the gridiron, newly marked with its chalk-lines was green under the autumn sun as a crowd of cadets released from drill and studies, flocked over the campus, shouting and laughing.

"Line up there, you scrubs!" called Paul Drew. "This is where we walk all over you. Here, Dick, catch this!" and he kicked a puzzling spiral toward the young millionaire.

Dick made a jump for the ball, but it slipped through his fingers.

"Wow! Rotten!" he cried. "That wouldn't do in a game."

"That's right," agreed Innis. "But you're no worse than the rest. Look at Watkins miss that drop kick he tried to make."

Shouts of derision from the scrub greeted the effort of Watkins to boot the pigskin. The scrub, in spite of its unenviable position, had been doing better in practice than the regular team. Captained by Tom Coleton the lads had scored many a touchdown on their superiors, and they were proud of it.

"Line up, fellows!" called Teddy Naylor, the Varsity captain. "We'll see what we can do."

The game at Kentfield was played under the old rules of halves, instead of quarters, and, in fact, all the teams in the Military League preferred that style.

Goals were chosen, and it was announced that two ten minute halves would be played. Dick was to play at quarter-back, John Stiver at left half-back, Ray Dutton at right half-back, Paul Drew at left guard, George Hall at right tackle, Teddy Naylor at full-back, Frank Rutley at left tackle, Jim Watkins at centre, Innis Beeby at right guard, Sam Porter as left end, and his crony, Jake Weston, at right end.

The scrub were to kick off, as Teddy wanted to see how well his men could rush back the ball. Not that he expected much, but somehow, under the stimulus of the new plan proposed by Dick, there was a more confident feeling among members of the Varsity eleven, than had existed in some time.

"I think we'll surprise 'em to-day," remarked Paul Drew, as he took his place beside Jim.

The signal was given, and Hal Foster made a big dent in the side of the ball. It came sailing toward the spread-out Varsity team, and was caught by Dick. He started back over the chalk marks, well protected by interference.

"Grab him! Don't let him get past you!" called Tom Coleton, who was in charge of the scrub. Dick's helpers shoved aside several impetuous lads who tried to break through to tackle him, and it looked as though he might make a sensational run. But when Bart Gerard slipped past Paul Drew, and got in to the running lad, there was a quick, fierce tackle, and Dick went down heavily.

"Not so bad! Line up!" cried Bert Cameron, who stole a few minutes from his studies to come out and see how the play was going.

"Get ready, fellows!" cried Dick, as he took his place behind Jim, while the big centre leaned over and prepared to snap back the ball when the signal was given.

Dick called out a string of numbers which indicated that Ray Dutton was to take the ball between the left guard and tackle of the scrub. The ball came back, and with all his might Dutton leaped for a hole that Beeby and Hall made for him. On and on he struggled pushing and being pushed.

"Brace, fellows! Brace!" implored Coleton, and his men tried, but there was no withstanding the fierce rush of the Varsity. Through they went, and when Dutton was finally stopped he had gained five yards.

"It's been some time since we did that," commented Dick, as he looked back at the ground covered—ground whereon were strewn fallen players for the rush had been a fierce one.

Again came the line up, and again the advance with the ball, Stiver taking it this time for a run around end. He made a good gain. Then followed more rushing tactics, until, when in reasonable distance of the goal, Dick gave the signal for a try for one from the field.

Straight and true the ball came back to Teddy Naylor, and the next instant it was booted over the crossbar.

"Wow!" cried Beeby capering about. "That's the stuff. Now if that was against Blue Hill I'd stand on my head!"

"Impossible, old chap—I mean impossible to stand on your head—you're not balanced right," panted Dick, for the last few minutes of play had been strenuous. "But it was good work all the same."

"You can't repeat it," declared Coleton, half chagrined yet glad that the Varsity was picking up.

But the Varsity did even better, for they rolled up two touchdowns in that half, a thing they had been unable to do since practice started.

They did not have things all their own way, however, for the scrub played so fiercely and with such desperate energy in the next half, that they, too, got a touchdown, and would have had another but for a splendid tackle Porter made.

"Good!" cried Teddy encouragingly, for Porter was not a good player, and would not train properly. But he had been picked on the team early in the season, when available material was scarce, and the captain did not like to drop him now. His fine stopping of the man with the ball, however, showed what he could do when he tried.

The play was resumed. There were only a few more minutes left, and the scrubs were trying with all their might to score again, while, on their part, the Varsity was trying to stop them. The scrub had the ball on the Varsity twenty-five yard line, when the signal came for a play through centre.

Dick half guessed that it was coming, and when the man with the ball made his appearance in the hole torn for him, our hero met him with a suddenness that shocked them both.

"I've got you!" cried the young millionaire. There was a revolving struggle, and then something hit Dick on the head. It became black all around him, and he went down in a limp heap, while he heard some one crying:

"Get up, fellows, Hamilton's hurt!"

CHAPTER V

DISQUIETING NEWS

There was a singing in Dick's ears. He seemed to be on a heaving, rolling sea, and he dimly wondered how he happened to be back on board a boat. Then he felt a dash of water on his face—cold, stinging water,—and he half imagined himself back on the raft with a sea breaking over him. Next he felt some one lifting him to his feet, and he heard the murmur of voices.

"That was a nasty blow."

"Yes. Who did it?"

"Shall we send for the doctor?"

"I'm—I'm all right," protested Dick feebly, as he opened his eyes. He came back to earth with a shock, and the boatlike motion suddenly ceased. "I—I——"

"Are you sure you're all right?" asked Paul anxiously.

Dick put his hand up to his head. A big lump was beginning to form, and was tender to the touch. His head started to ache and hum.

"That was my fault," contritely confessed Hal Foster, of the scrub. "I was trying to stop you from making that tackle, when my feet slipped from under me, and shot right at your head, Hamilton. I hope you're not much hurt. I'm awfully sorry."

He took hold of Dick's arm in a brotherly fashion.

"It's all right—don't mention it old chap. It was no one's fault. I shouldn't have jumped in so quickly. I'm all right again. Come on, we'll finish the game."

"No, the time's about up," announced Teddy. "We've had enough for to-day. And it's been better practice than we've had in a long while. I guess we're all anxious to get on Hamilton's team."

"Hamilton's team?" asked Sam Porter, in a curious tone. "Since when has it been *his* eleven?"

"Oh, I forgot you hadn't heard the news," went on Teddy. "Why Dick is going to pay for two of the best coaches in the country, and we're going to have a team as *is* a team. That's why we all played so well to-day, I guess—even the scrub."

"Thanks!" exclaimed Tom Coleton. "We'll do you up good and proper to-morrow just the same."

"Not with Dick Hamilton's team," cried Teddy with a laugh.

"It isn't going to be my team at all," declared Dick, as he supported himself on Paul's shoulder and walked along, after his head had again been bathed in the cold water. "I don't want it known as that. I'm only doing what any fellow would do—putting up some cash to help out. It isn't my team at all."

"I should say not!" sneered Porter. "Hamilton's team—that sounds like playing favorites all right."

"Yes, if it keeps on this will be known as the Kentfield-Hamilton Military Academy," added his crony.

Dick heard, and his face flushed. He took a step toward the two lads, but he was unsteady on his feet, for the blow on his head had been severe.

"You'll have to take that back Mr. Porter," said our hero a bit stiffly, "and you too, Mr. Weston."

It was seldom that the cadets addressed each other thus, and only when there was some feeling engendered.

"Take what back?" demanded Porter.

"What you said about favorites," went on Dick. "I won't stand for that."

There was that in his look and manner, and in his words that impressed not only his friends but the two cronies as well. They realized that Dick as an upper classman, had considerable influence, and, though they had their own following, due to their wealth and their willingness to spend money, they doubtless felt that they had gone too far.

"Oh, well, I didn't mean anything," said Porter, half sulkily. "I—I was only joking."

"I don't like such jokes," declared Dick grimly, and he looked at Weston.

"Same here," muttered Porter's crony. "I was only fooling."

"Your apologies are accepted," was Dick's reply. He walked on, half supported by Paul, and when his chums saw how evidently weak he was they wanted him to go to the doctor's office. But Dick would not.

"I'll be all right in the morning," he said. "All I need is a little rest. We're getting right into football good and proper," he added with an attempt at a smile.

"Yes, starting off with a hospital list," added Teddy. "Don't have too much of it, though."

Dick was rather lame and stiff the next morning, and his head was in poor shape for study, so he cut some lectures, and got excused from drill and artillery practice. In the afternoon however, he was much better, and insisted on going through light practice in signals playing one half against the scrub, his place being taken by a substitute in the second period.

Whether it was because Dick was off the team, or because the scrub played with fiercer energy, due to their defeat of the day before, was not manifested, but the Varsity was beaten by a score of fourteen to eleven, and once more there was a feeling of gloom in the ranks of the first eleven.

"Oh, it's all right," Teddy assured his players. "We will make up for it to-morrow. By the way, Dick, when are your coaches coming?"

"I've written, and I expect an answer some time this week. It may take a little longer than I hoped, but I told them not to let money stand in the way. I have made an offer to Burke Martin of Yale, and Wilson Spencer of Princeton."

"Martin and Spencer!" cried Teddy in delight. "Say, if we get them here they'll make even the goal posts play the game. There aren't any two better coaches living."

"It pays to get the best," said Dick, with a smile. "I have had my father send a line to the athletic committee of the Tigers, and I told him to write to our distant relative who once went to Yale, and get him to put in a good word for us."

"Fine!" cried the captain. "I fancy they'll make the team all over again when they get here. I may lose my place."

"Nonsense!" declared Dick. "But the way I feel about it is this—we want the best men to represent Kentfield, and we'll let the coaches do the picking. I don't want to play unless they say I'm better, in my particular place, than some other fellow. It's a fair field and no favor for me."

"Same here," declared Naylor. "I'll step out the minute I'm asked to. It's for the honor of Kentfield, not for any particular player. But it would be rubbing it in if they turned you down Dick, after what you've done—putting up all that money."

"Say, look here, that's a matter I want to speak about!" exclaimed Dick with sudden energy. "I don't want the coaches to know who is putting up the money—I don't want it known that I am doing it. They are both fair men, and I know you couldn't influence them with a million dollars. But let this matter be kept quiet, and have it given out that the athletic committee of Kentfield is supplying the funds. Then there can't be anything said against me."

"I guess that would be the best way," assented Teddy. "I'll call a meeting right away and we'll settle it. But you say you have already written to the coaches."

"I did, but I wrote in the name of the committee," said Dick. "I took that liberty, as I wanted to conceal my part in the affair. I thought it would be all right."

"Sure. I'll see that it is."

The athletic committee at a meeting that night, endorsed the action of our hero, and the members were bound to secrecy in the matter as to who was supplying the money with which to pay the coaches.

For the next few days practice went on, and there was a distinct improvement in the playing of the Varsity team, to the disquieting of the scrub, for those unfortunate players were shoved all over the gridiron, and several were laid up with bruises, as the first eleven was playing for touchdowns, and secured several. Still their playing was anything but what it should be, and the lads themselves realized it. But they were willing to learn, and anxiously awaited the arrival of the coaches.

Dick, meanwhile, had spent some time with Porter and his crony, though he did not like their companionship. He played many games of pool and billiards with them, losing occasionally, and again, by some brilliant cue work, making the two gasp with astonishment and chagrin.

"I don't see how it is that you don't win oftener," spoke Porter a bit suspiciously one day.

"Oh, well, it's luck I guess," declared Dick, and then he steered the conversation around to the topic on which he wanted information—the plan to wrest the control of the trolley line from his father.

But Porter either did not want to tell more, or could not. He declared that his father's plans were coming along in great shape, and that Mr. Porter was a wonder as a financier.

"There'll be some surprised millionaires when my dad gets through with them," he boasted.

"Is he doing it all alone—I mean hasn't he some men associated with him?" asked Dick as carelessly as he could as he made a neat carom shot.

"Oh, I guess there are some pikers in along with my governor, but he's the main squeeze," declared Porter. "He lets some fellows trail along so he can use 'em when he wants to. But he gets most of the dough, and he keeps it too. I hope the deal soon goes through, for I want my allowance increased, and the governor promised to raise the ante as soon as he gets control of this electric road. By the way, it's somewhere out your way, Hamilton. You must have heard of it."

"I have," answered Dick as quietly as before.

"Is your dad interested? I hear he has scads of money. Maybe he's in with my father."

"No, I fancy not. It's your turn, Weston," and Dick turned aside to conceal a grim smile on his face.

That night there was a letter for Dick from his father. It contained disquieting news, for it bore the information that the enemies of the millionaire were getting more active.

"There is some other man besides Mr. Porter who is in this matter," wrote Mr. Hamilton. "I can't just learn who he is, but he holds a large number of shares, that he has bought up in little lots from the original holders. If I could learn who he is, and get in touch with him, I might persuade him to sell me some stock, so I would have the controlling interest. Then I could bid these others defiance. If you can learn who this man is, Dick wire me at once. I'll do the same for you, but as things are now they certainly look bad for the Hamilton family. But keep up your spunk."

"Poor dad," mused Dick, "I guess managing finances is about as hard as trying to re-shape a slumping football team. But we'll both do our best. I wonder who that unknown man is?"

CHAPTER VI

MR. DUNCASTER AGAIN

"I say, Dick, are you in?"

It was a cautious voice making this inquiry after a gentle knock at the door of the room where our hero and Paul Drew lived when they were not playing football, drilling with the other cadets, or reciting their lessons.

"Who is it?" whispered Dick to his chum.

"Blessed if I know. Sounds like Beeby, and again it might be Teddy. Going to let him in?"

"Sure. No one's around this early and it's safe. Unbolt the door. I've done enough boning to-night."

It was shortly after Dick had received the letter from his father, in which the disquieting news was given, and the two cadets were preparing their lessons for the morrow.

But as this was ever-wearying work, to be disposed of as quickly as possible in case any pleasure was available, the two friends welcomed the disturbing knock.

"Come on in," invited our hero as his chum opened the portal. "What's up, anyhow."

"Something doing," replied Innis Beeby cheerfully as he slid inside the room, and carefully closed the door. "Are you fellows ready for a little fun?"

"It depends on what kind," answered Dick. "Are you going to run one of the six-pounders up on the chapel steps, or turn the flag upside down?"

"Neither. But did you know that Porter and Weston were giving a little spread to-night?"

"A spread? No! And those fellows only freshmen of the freshest kind," answered Paul. "Say, we ought to take 'em down a peg."

"Exactly what I think," agreed Beeby. "I came over to see if you didn't want to join in the fun. We're going to invade their spread, take Porter and Weston captive, and carry them into town."

"Then what?" inquired Paul eagerly. He was always ready for fun.

"We'll make them do 'sentry-go' in front of the town jail. Have them march up and down with wooden guns on their shoulders. Maybe they won't feel sick!"

"But will they do it?" asked Paul.

"They'll have to if we make a freshman matter of it. Otherwise they'll go to Coventry for the rest of the term. Oh, they'll do it all right. How about it, Dick?"

Now our hero had shown a curious lack of interest in the matter of hazing Porter and Weston, from the time their names were mentioned. He seemed to cool down all at once, though he had always done his share heretofore in making the first year men feel their inferior positions.

"Well?" asked Innis Beeby, after a pause, as he glanced at the young millionaire.

"Oh, what's the use?" inquired Dick. "Can't we let 'em alone? It might make trouble in the football team if we put them through the third degree too strong."

"Bosh!" cried Innis. "They need it. Besides, if any fellows take offense at a little hazing they're not fit to play on the football team. Eh, Paul?"

"Sure not."

But Dick was thinking what effect his participation in the affair would have, especially when he still wanted to get some information from Porter, and depended on keeping in with that worthy in order to secure it.

"Come along, Dick," urged Innis.

"Oh, I don't know," and the young millionaire paused before a case full of books—a case seldom opened. "I ought to do some boning, and——"

"What!" cried Beeby aghast. "Don't speak of such a thing again. You nearly gave me heart disease. Come along and have some fun. We don't often have a chance at it, but there is a faculty pow-wow to-night, and the coast is unusually clear. That's why Porter had his spread I guess. We'll go over, make a rough house, and take him and his friend out for an airing. Then we'll all feel better. Come on, Dick."

There was no help for it, and, somewhat against his will, our hero made ready to accompany his chums. He did not like to go, as he feared to get on bad terms with Porter.

It was a very much surprised party of surreptitious midnight feasters on which our hero and his chums burst half an hour later. The spread was being held in the apartments of Porter, for he had hired a sitting room as well as a dormitory chamber. Both were well filled with most of the members of the "sporting" set.

"What does this mean?" demanded Porter indignantly, as the upper classmen made their appearance. "I think I did not invite you to my little affair."

"No, we didn't wait for a bid, Porter, though it was mighty careless of you to overlook us," retorted Beeby. "But we came, anyhow. Now I guess you can come with us, Porter and Weston. We're going to initiate you into the mysteries of the gun club."

There were significant glances from the other cadets for they knew what this meant. Many of them had been through it on previous occasions.

"We're not coming!" exclaimed Porter aggressively.

"No, and you haven't any right to interrupt us in this manner," declared his crony with dignity. "Leave here at once."

"With you, dear friend, and not otherwise," put in Teddy Naylor. "Come on, it's part of the game."

But Porter and Weston could not see it that way. They protested, and made a show of fighting. They appealed to the other cadets, but the latter said they had better comply with the demands of the upper classmen.

Even then the two cronies remained ugly, and made a show of resistance, until Beeby and the others, tired of the delay, made a sudden rush, tied the captives with ropes that had been brought for the purpose, and marched them quietly from the building.

"Here, you let go of that rope, Hamilton!" cried Porter, as he saw Dick holding one end of the cords that bound the hands of the two captives together.

"Can't do it—nohow," was the grim answer, and yet Dick wished that he might, for he was afraid that this would prove an insurmountable barrier to future talks with the son of the man who was seeking to ruin Mr. Hamilton.

"Then I'll get even with you," threatened Porter. "I'll make you fellows sorry for this night's work, you see if I don't."

"Don't mind him—he's talking like a cannon-swab," said Beeby with a chuckle.

In a little while the two captives had been placed in front of the town jail, with instructions to march up and down before it, bearing on their shoulders grotesque wooden guns made for the hazing purpose.

"And if you desert inside of an hour, you know what it means," threatened Jim Watkins. "You'll belong to the Down and Out Club after that. So keep on the job."

Porter and Weston knew better than to disobey, for their chums, who had been present at the spread, had whispered to them of the dire penalties that would follow a disregard of the hazing instructions of the upper classmen. So the two cronies marched gravely up and down the dark street, while occasional pedestrians paused to gaze, chuckle silently as they realized what was in progress.

"I'm not going to stand it!" indignantly declared Porter after a half hour of the ordeal.

"We'd better," counseled Weston. "I don't want to stay at Kentfield for a month with not a soul to speak to but you. We've got to do it."

"All right. But I'll get even with Hamilton for this. I think he started it. I'll get square with him."

"Same here," and Weston shifted his gun to the other shoulder, and marched forward wearily.

The night wore on, and in the shadows of several buildings the upper classmen who had originated the joke on the two freshmen, looked on and chuckled in mirth. Occasionally they called out a remark to the sentries. More people passed, and some paused to laugh, to the anger of Porter and Weston. Policemen walked by, but they were familiar with that form of hazing and did not make any complaint of the odd sight. Some of the prisoners in the jail peered out from their barred windows and jeered. All this was bitterness to the two.

After a time Beeby and his chums wearied of the joke, and on the invitation of George Hall went to a nearby soda fountain for some chocolate.

"They'll skip out as soon as we're gone," declared Ray Dutton.

"No, I think they'll stick," declared Innis. "Anyhow, Dick, you go back and take a look. We'll keep your chocolate for you."

Our hero did not relish the task, but did not want to object. Accordingly, he walked back to the corner where he could look down the street and catch a glimpse of the two cadet jail-sentries. They were still on their posts.

Dick turned back to join his chums, and, as did so he almost collided with a man coming around the corner in an opposite direction.

"I beg your pardon!" exclaimed the cadet. "I didn't see you."

"Very evidently," was the rasping reply. "That's the trouble with you young men, you never look where you're going. Ah! I see, another one of the soldiers—and if it isn't the same one who nearly ran me down the other night in an automobile."

Dick recognized the aged Mr. Duncaster.

"I—I'm afraid it is," our hero faltered. "I—I didn't mean to, I'm sure. I didn't hurt you this time."

"No, but it's not your fault that you didn't. You came around that corner under a full head of steam. Have you run down any more persons in your auto?" Enos Duncaster asked sarcastically.

"No, and that time it wasn't my fault."

"Hum—let's see—your name is Hamilton—son of Mortimer Hamilton—I know him—a hard man in a bargain. Well, I'll let you off this time. Who are those two young men marching up and down over there—chums of yours?"

"Yes—we—we're hazing them," faltered Dick.

"Ha! Hazing! A senseless and foolish proceeding! But just what I would expect of you soldier lads—heartless and cruel. Well, let me pass, I've wasted enough time on you."

Mr. Duncaster's voice was grim and harsh. He brushed by Dick roughly and passed on down the street, muttering to himself about the foolishness of youths in general, and in particular regarding those boys who attended military schools.

Dick, having assured himself that the hazed ones were still patrolling their post, returned to his chums and helped get away with some chocolate soda.

There was a telegram awaiting our hero when he reached his room later that night, Porter and Weston having been released from their hazing duties.

"Hum, I guess that's from dad," mused Dick. "I wonder what the new developments are?"

Rapidly he scanned the few words. They were these:

"Dear Dick: Enos Duncaster is the name of the man who holds a lot of trolley stock. See if you can locate him for me. I understand he lives somewhere in the vicinity of your academy. Trouble is thickening. I need help."

"Whew!" whistled Dick. "Enos Duncaster! He's the man who holds the stock, and whom both sides are after. And I'm in his bad books if ever a fellow was! Whew! I can see the finish of this without any spectacles!"

CHAPTER VII

THE COACHES ARRIVE

Cavalry evolutions were ordered for the next day, followed by a field drill, and a service march of several miles, so that there was no chance for football practice.

"And we need all we can get, too," remarked Dick to Paul.

"Let's suggest to Colonel Masterly that he give up lessons and drill while the gridiron season is on," suggested Paul with a smile.

"Yes, I can see him doing it," cried the young millionaire. "Which horse are you going to ride, Paul?"

"The little black—I'm fond of him, though he is a bit vicious."

The boys were on their way to the cavalry barracks, and in their wake, and ahead of them, were other cadets hastening to secure their mounts, for the bugle was impatiently calling.

"Do you think Spitfire is safe?" asked Dick, naming the steed Paul had said he would use. "Why don't you take the little gray I used to ride? He's a good steady mount, though a bit slow."

"That's the trouble," was the answer, as Dick's roommate tightened the belt of his sabre. "I want to keep up with the rest of the bunch. No, I'll take Spitfire. I reckon you'll ride Rex; eh?"

"Sure," for Dick had brought his own fine horse to Kentfield with him, together with his bulldog, and Grit was now ambling along behind the two chums, occasionally uttering a low bark of satisfaction, for the dog loved to go along on the practice "hikes."

"Well, be careful," cautioned the wealthy youth, as Paul went in to saddle up.

"All right," laughed his chum, but there was a serious look on the face of our hero, and he resolved to keep near his chum that day.

Artillery practice followed the cavalry drill, and the cadets, sitting as straight as ramrods on the caissons while the horses galloped around at full speed, leaped off the moment the sudden halt was made, unlimbered, fired rapid shots and, limbering up again, went off at a mad gallop to repeat the operation.

"Forward march!" signalled the bugler when arrangements had been made for the "hike," and the eager horses, astride of which were the no less eager cadets, started off.

It was a pleasant day, though a trifle cool, and the service overcoats, with their flashily yellow linings, showing gaily in the sun when they flapped back, felt very comfortable.

At first the march was in orderly array, while Major Webster, and some of the other military instructors, passed here and there among the new cadets, telling them the proper way to manage their horses. Dick and his chums, however, having passed several terms at the academy, needed no hints.

"Don't hold your snaffle reins that way, Mr. Porter," said the major to the new lad as he rode up beside him. "You can't control your horse in an emergency. Let me show you," which he did, also correcting a fault he noticed in the way Weston sat on his steed.

"Humph! I guess I know something about horses," complained Porter, when the instructors had passed on. "I straddled one before I came here. I had a German riding master, and what he didn't know about horses wasn't worth putting on ice. I'll ride as I please."

As he spoke, he put spurs to his horse, digging them in viciously, and as the startled animal leaped forward, the cruel lad wrenched the poor brute's mouth open with the strong curb bit. There was a momentary confusion among the horses immediately surrounding Porter, and several of the older cadets called sharply to him to "stop his funny work."

"Oh, you fellows make me tired!" Porter grumbled. "Why don't you do some fast riding."

"You'll get all the fast riding you want if you stay long enough," spoke Paul sharply.

A little later the order was given to ride at will, and Major Webster, galloping back to Dick, said:

"Captain Hamilton, you and Lieutenant Drew take several of the new cadets and ride around by the long lake road. Give them some points. Take about ten—Mr. Porter and Mr. Weston, fall in with Captain Hamilton's squad."

"Hum! I guess Captain Hamilton thinks he knows it all," sneered Weston.

"Not a bit of it," answered Dick good naturedly. "But orders are orders you'll find. Come ahead, and I'll show you a fine bit of road, some magnificent scenery, and we'll have a good gallop. Look out there, Paul, I don't like the way Spitfire is acting!" The young millionaire called this suddenly as he saw his chum's steed waltzing up to another animal, with ears laid back as though to bite, and so cause trouble.

"I can manage him," answered Paul confidently, as he put the restless steed about in a rapid circle.

Dick's little squad, himself and Paul the only really military experienced riders in it, set off along a cross road that would bring them to the shore path of Lake Wagatook. There, as the young captain had said, was a fine road with scenery that one would have to travel many miles to equal.

"Now for some fast riding!" called Dick, when they came to a long open stretch. "You can go as far as you like, Porter."

"Good! Then here I go!"

Viciously he again spurred his horse, and his example was followed by his crony. The two animals sprang away together, but Porter's stepped on a round stone, stumbled, and almost fell. The boastful lad proved that he did know something about animals, for he pulled up the beast's head sharply, and got him in hand again. Not before, however, the frightened steed had collided with some force into Spitfire.

Paul's horse lashed out instantly with its hind hoofs, and then, with a shake of the head bolted. The cadet attempted to pull him in, but, a moment later, uttered a startled cry.

"My curb rein is broken!"

It flashed through Dick's head in an instant what that meant. Naturally ugly, Spitfire, now unusually frightened, was practically beyond control. Paul was doing his best but was rapidly being carried down the broad highway, with Porter and Weston galloping after him, their own steeds none too well in hand.

"I've got to stop him!" exclaimed Dick. "I've got to catch Spitfire and stop him, or Paul may be hurt! That brute isn't fit to ride. Come, Rex!"

Rex needed no spur. Off he started like a racer, and Dick, looking back, flung over his shoulder at the other cadets:

"Come on, fellows, keep up as well as you can!"

Rex soon fell into his stride, and fairly skimmed along the smooth road. But Paul was quite a distance ahead, and Spitfire was running hard. Dick could see his chum sitting easily in the saddle, now and then leaning forward trying to grasp the broken and flapping end of the curb rein.

"Don't do it! Wait! I'll catch you!" shouted Dick, but it is doubtful if Paul heard him.

"Come on, Rex old man, we must do better than this. We can beat Spitfire," spoke Dick gently, patting his horse on the neck. Rex understood and let out a few more "kinks" of his speed.

The young millionaire soon reached and passed Porter and Weston, whose steeds had soon tired of the speedy spurt. But not so with Spitfire. Dick knew he would have a race. On galloped Rex, and before him sped Spitfire.

"A little better, boy, a little better," urged Dick. And a little better Rex went.

Dick could now see that he was overhauling the uncontrolled steed, and he was glad of it, for he feared Paul might be flung off, in spite of the lad's skill in horsemanship.

"I'll have him in another minute," reflected Dick, when there suddenly loomed in sight a big touring car, and right at a point where the road narrowed. Spitfire was viciously shaking his head, now and then holding it low.

"Jove, he'll crash into that car!" cried Dick aloud. "Why don't they keep that infernal horn still? It's making him wilder," for the autoists were frantically tooting away.

"I've got to get in ahead of him, and ride him off to one side," thought our hero. "Rex, old boy, I hate to do it, but—just a touch."

Gently Dick pricked his pet animal with the spurs—just a touch, for voice was not quite incentive enough. Like a shot Rex sprang forward, and covered the ground so rapidly that in another brief instant the young millionaire was ahead of his friend, and between Spitfire and the now stationary auto. Then, with the skill of long practice, Dick urged Rex up to Spitfire, who was losing speed, and a moment later the frightened steed had been forced off the road, into the grassy side path, and headed toward a fence, which effectually stopped farther progress.

"Well ridden! Excellently well ridden!" cried the man at the wheel of the auto. Dick saluted, for there were several ladies in the car, and then turned to Paul.

"All right, old man," he asked anxiously.

"Yes, but I might not have been a little later. I should have looked to my reins. Thanks—for coming as you did," and Paul warmly grasped Dick's hand.

"You knew I'd come. Now let's see if we can mend that leather and ride back. Are you game?"

"Oh, sure. I fancy Spitfire has had all he wanted for to-day." In fact the animal was much subdued after his run. The auto passed on, not even the tooting of the horn causing Paul's steed to prance. Then he and Dick managed to patch up the curb leather, and rode back to meet the other cadets.

"Don't spur up so suddenly when other horses are too near you," advised the young captain to Porter, who seemed a bit ashamed of the trouble he had caused.

"I beg your pardon, old man—and yours, Captain," spoke the lad, who though impulsive, was not a bad fellow at heart.

"All right," answered Dick easily. "We'll take it a little more slowly now."

They finished the ride in about two hours, reaching the academy as the last of the other riding squads came in. Dick made no report of the little incident which, but for his promptness, might have had a fatal, or at least a serious, ending.

Rifle practice, and field telegraph work occupied the rest of the day, and there was a final drill and inspection in the late afternoon.

"A pretty strenuous day," remarked Paul to Dick, as they went to their room that evening.

"Yes, and there'll be another to-morrow."

"How so?"

"We must get in some good football practice, for I expect the two coaches soon, perhaps to-day."

"Then Martin and Spencer are both coming?"

"Yes, the good salary and the influence of the old grads, including dad, brought them around."

"I'm glad of it. Now Kentfield will do something."

Out on the gridiron were a score or more of the mole-skin clad warriors, doing all sorts of things to a harmless pigskin spheroid. It was booted and passed about.

"Line up! Line up!" called Teddy Naylor. "Get together fellows! Where are you scrubs? We're going to send all of you to the hospital. Come on, Dick, run through some signals."

Eleven panting youths faced eleven others, and the ball went sailing into the midst of the Varsity. George Hall caught it, and ran back with it, well protected by interference. But some of the scrub managed to get through, and downed him before he had gone far.

"Down!" panted George, as he tried to rise from underneath a mound of human forms.

"Down indeed, but too soon," remarked a strange voice, to one side of the scrimmaging lads. They all looked up. Two young men stood looking at the heap of humanity. They were strangers to all the cadets.

"May I ask—perhaps you don't know it, but only members of the academy are allowed out here," spoke Teddy Naylor a bit stiffly.

"Oh, but we were sent for," remarked one of the strangers. "We just came, and we were interested in seeing you play."

"You were sent for?" repeated the captain.

"Yes, that is——"

"Oh, isn't this Mr. Martin?" asked Dick, striding forward and holding out his hand.

"Yes," was the answer from the man with a small black moustache. "I'm Mr. Martin and this is Mr. Spencer," and he indicated his companion.

"Fellows, the coaches have come!" cried Dick. "Now to learn how to play football!"

CHAPTER VIII

THE TRY-OUT

Scores of expectant lads sat in the meeting room of the Kentfield Academy gymnasium. They faced two quiet gentlemen, who, from time to time, whispered to each other. Beside the two gentlemen were Teddy Naylor and Innis Beeby, who also, as the minutes passed, conferred in low voices.

"Hadn't we better start?" asked Innis, of the football captain.

"No, we'll wait a few minutes longer. Porter and Weston aren't here, and I want them to come."

"Those fellows will never train for the eleven."

"Yes they will. There is good material in both of them. Here they are now. I guess we've got enough. Will you start her off, or shall I?"

"Oh, you'd better, Teddy. I'll say something later if it's necessary. Better introduce 'em formally first, and let 'em do most of the talking," and the stout cadet looked at the two coaches.

"Fellows," began Teddy, arising and moving forward a bit nervously, "you all know why we are here—that is I suppose—we are here—we came——"

"Good, Teddy!" called someone encouragingly. "Say it over, we missed part of it."

"We are here——"

"Because we're here!" interpolated another tormentor.

"Oh, hang it all! We've met to discuss football!" cried the captain in desperation. "The athletic committee feels that something should be done—you all know how Blue Hill turned us down—we've got to play better. We now have two of the best coaches in the country, and they're going to have charge. I take pleasure in introducing to you Mr. Burke Martin of Yale, and Mr. Wilson Spencer of Princeton."

"Three cheers for both of 'em!" cried someone, and the big gymnasium reverberated with the shouts. Mr. Martin nodded to his colleague to speak first, and the Princeton coach arose.

"I am glad to see you all so enthusiastic," he began. "You know why the services of Mr. Martin and myself were secured, and I assure you that we will do our best to get your team into shape. To do this we may have to tell you some unpleasant truths, and some of you who imagine yourself good players may find that you cannot make the team—at least not at once. But I hope there will be no hard feelings. Now to begin with, I want to say something about training, as that is my specialty, and afterward Mr. Martin will give you a little talk about playing the game to win."

Thereupon the Princeton coach touched briefly on the more important points of the training system. It was soon evident to the Kentfield lads that they had not done enough of this in times past, and perhaps this was the cause of some of their defeats—at least they ascribed it to that.

"Football men, among other things, need quickness," said Mr. Spencer, "and beyond all else, according to Michael Murphy of Pennsylvania, than whom there is no better trainer, the players on the gridiron need to have plenty of superfluous energy to draw on. That is you need a sort of reserve stock to use at the time of a big match. Your mental condition is no less important than your physical. You must *want* to win, and you must feel that you are *going* to win.

"The care a player takes of himself in the summer determines in a great measure how soon he can get into condition in the fall."

"We had pretty good training on Dick's yacht," whispered Innis to Teddy.

"Now, I propose that we start at the beginning," went on the coach. "We'll have some setting-up exercises, some track work, and general gymnastics, and then we'll get in a position to pick the men for the Varsity by a series of try-outs." He made some special references to the details of training, and then yielded to Mr. Martin.

The latter went into the fine points of the game, emphasizing the needs of the individual players, laying stress on what the backs, tackles, ends and guards should do, and urging on the lads the necessity for fast, snappy playing.

"Demoralize your opponents by the quickness with which you jump into formations," said the Yale man. "As soon as one play is finished be ready for the next. In defense, never give up, no matter how the game seems to be going against you. Hold hard, tire out the other side, and then you may have a chance to get the ball and—win!"

He spoke at some length, and his remarks were eagerly listened to. Then Innis got up, and, after a trifling show of nervousness, and two or three false starts, which gave the cadets a chance to "rig" him, he said:

"I want to say that I'm sure none of us will feel any resentment if, after a fair trial, it is decided by the two new coaches that he isn't fit for the team," went on the stout lad. "I know my own failings and I'll be trying to get my weight down———"

"Don't eat so much," urged Jim Watkins, and there was a laugh, whereat Innis blushed.

"And I'm going to train hard," he concluded. "I guess that will be all this evening."

The meeting broke up, but the boys lingered to talk with each other, many surrounding the coaches, and asking all sorts of questions.

It had been arranged with Colonel Masterly that Mr. Martin and Mr. Spencer could occupy rooms in the Senior dormitory, and Dick, through the athletic committee, had provided for paying the bills.

Preliminary work of training started the next day, and though some of the boys thought it useless, they went through the exercises. But the two coaches were too wise to keep the cadets at mere gymnasium work too long, and so some field work with the ball, and some running exercises, were arranged.

Several candidates could not stand the pace and the grind and dropped out, but their places were eagerly taken by others. The scrub members were enthusiastic, and each one hoped to make the Varsity.

"Now we'll try a little practice game, between the first and second teams," proposed Mr. Martin, about a week after the arrival of himself and his colleague. "It will be in the nature of a try-out, for probably those who do the best work will be put in the first squad, and from that the men for the Varsity will be picked. That does not mean, however, that those who fail to make good this time will be barred. We will keep on the lookout for good material all the while."

"And I want you boys to feel that you are always being watched," added Mr. Spencer. "We'll have our eyes on you when you least expect it."

"That's what we want," declared Dick with a laugh. "We want the best team possible."

"Yes—Hamilton's team," sneered Porter to Weston.

"He'll be sure to make it, anyhow," added the latter.

"If he does, and I don't, I'll kick up a row," threatened the rich lad.

"So will I. Come on let's go to town and have a pool game. I'm pretty dry, too.

"Better not get caught with any of that bottled stuff," cautioned Porter.

"Don't worry. They will have to be pretty foxy to spot me, but I'm not going to be a temperance crank just because those coaches say so. Come ahead and we'll have some fun. It will be stiff enough work to-morrow."

The practice game was a hard one. Each player did his best, and on several occasions, after a hard scrimmage, time had to be taken out while some cadet had the wind pumped back into him, or a twisted ankle vigorously rubbed.

Slowly but surely the Varsity pushed back the luckless scrub. Slowly but surely a touchdown seemed about to be made. Dick gave a signal for a fake kick. John Stiver, the left half-back was to take the ball, run wide toward his own right end, pass the pigskin to Teddy Naylor, at full-back and the latter was to try and advance it for a touchdown.

All went well until Teddy got the ball. Then, as he was charging around the end, with Dick and Stiver forming interference for him, he dropped the ball. Something like a groan came from the young millionaire, for he saw their chance to score lost. Tom Coleton, of the scrub, came charging through, but the next instant Dick had made a grab for the pigskin, picked it up, and, dodging Coleton, made a dash toward the goal line.

The day was saved, for our hero, making a splendid run, planted the ball squarely between the posts, and behind the final chalk mark.

"Touchdown! Touchdown!" came the triumphant cry. "Varsity touchdown!"

"But it wouldn't have been one except for Hamilton," remarked Mr. Martin grimly. "Naylor, how did it happen that you couldn't hold the ball?"

"I don't know," answered the luckless captain.

"We can't have that," remarked Mr. Spencer with a dubious shake of his head. "Well, try for goal."

It was an easy shot, and Innis made it quickly. Then the game went on, but the Varsity could not score again, and the scrub was equally unable to advance the ball when they had it.

"That will be enough for to-day," announced the coaches. "We are going to make some changes to-morrow. The list of the first squad will be posted in the gym."

There were anxious looks among the players. Who would be on the preliminary Varsity team. It was a question every cadet asked himself.

"Well, if I don't make it," reflected Dick, "I will have so much more time to try and get on the trail of Mr. Duncaster. But—I want to play football."

CHAPTER IX

THE ACCUSATION

"Come on, Dick!" cried Paul excitedly, as he burst into the room where his chum was industriously boning away over the pages of his trigonometry. "Hurry up!"

"What's the rush, son?" calmly asked the young millionaire.

"Haven't you heard? The list of the Varsity players has just been posted in the gym."

"Who told you?"

"Toots. He was whistling 'Just Before the Battle, Mother,' when I spotted him, and he sung out that the list was up. I want to see if my name is there."

"It sure is—you played your head off yesterday," declared Dick.

"That's no sure sign. I wish I had your chances."

"Nonsense!" exclaimed Dick. Yet, deep down in his heart he could not help feeling that perhaps, after all, he might be put on the scrub. He had played his best, but he had made some errors, and one fumble. Yet it would seem that his run and touchdown would count for much.

"Aren't you ever coming?" asked Paul. "Jove! I can't wait."

"Sure I'm coming," answered his roommate, as he tossed the book upon a heap of others. "No use getting excited though."

It was the day after the try-out game, and the coaches after a long and none too easy process of elimination had arrived at some definite results. They had made up a tentative Varsity team.

As Dick and Paul hurried across the campus toward the gymnasium, they saw many other students bent on the same errand as themselves, for the news had quickly spread, and each cadet who had football aspirations was anxious to see if he was one of the lucky eleven.

There was such a crowd about the bulletin board that for a time Dick and his chum could not get near it. They heard many names called out though, for the second team was posted as well as the first.

"There's Beeby—lucky dog—he's made it!" exclaimed someone.

"I thought he was too fat," came in disappointed tones from Roy Haskell, who coveted the centre rush's place.

"And Hall—he's on."

"Yes, and there's Dutton and Stiver, both on the first team."

"Say—look—Teddy hasn't made it!"

"Get out!"

"Sure not! Look, he's on the scrub."

"Poor Teddy. That's because of that fumble yesterday. Who's got his place?"

"I can't see. Oh, yes, it's Coleton!"

"Say, did you hear that?" asked Paul in a low voice of his chum.

"Yes, it's bad news. But Teddy will be on before we get through the season. He's a better all around player than Coleton. Can you get up there now?"

"I guess so. Come on. Say, let a fellow up, will you?" begged Paul of those about him.

As they were worming their way up they heard another piece of news.

"Porter is off," remarked one lad.

"I thought he'd be," came from Jim Watkins. "He made two bad fumbles yesterday, and he isn't quick enough for an end."

"Can you see, Dick?" asked Paul, as he clung to the side of his companion. "Is your name there."

"I don't know yet—Hey, Frank, get your head out of my way for a second; will you?"

"Sure thing, Dick. Tough about Teddy; isn't it?"

"Yes, but don't worry. We'll have him back."

"I hope so."

"Now can you see?" implored Paul.

"Yes, your name——"

Dick paused a moment.

"Well!" panted his roommate.

"Is there all right. You're on the Varsity."

"What position?"

"Left guard—where you wanted to play."

"But what about you, Dick?"

"Oh, I'm down at quarter all right," and from the calm way in which he said it those who heard him would never have imagined that Dick's heart had almost stopped beating when, for a brief moment, he thought he had caught sight of his name on the second list.

"Good, old man!" cried Paul fervently as he clasped his chum's hand. "I knew you'd make it. Now we'll see what sort of a team we'll have with the two changes. Are those the only ones made?"

"Yes, Porter and Naylor are off."

"Who's got Porter's place?"

"Hal Foster—a good fellow, too."

The throng surged about the bulletin board, newcomers arriving every minute, and all the cadets making various observations as they were pleased or disappointed. Teddy Naylor was not in sight. He had heard the news, and in the bitterness of his heart he kept to himself for a while.

Yet he did not complain. Teddy played the game fairly, and he was a loyal son of Kentfield. He was willing to defer to the judgment of the coaches—yet no one but himself knew how he longed to be among the first squad, and with a grim setting of his lips he resolved to make it before the big games were played.

"Well, come on," invited Paul to Dick. "I'll treat you to a soda on the strength of this."

"Don't you think it will put us out of training?"

"One can't. We've got to celebrate in some way."

The two chums strolled across the campus arm in arm, toward a spot where an enterprising dealer, well aware of the desire for sweets on the part of the students, had set up a little confectionery shop.

As Paul and his chum neared it they saw, walking toward them, Porter and Weston. The cronies were talking earnestly together.

"I wonder if Porter's heard?" ventured Paul.

"If he hasn't he soon will. I'm sorry for him. He's a brilliant player, but careless. He may come back before the season is over."

"He isn't much of an addition to the team—too snobby for me," spoke Paul in a low voice.

Porter suddenly seemed to become aware of Dick's presence, for Weston called his attention to it. Glancing up quickly, a black look passed over the features of the rich youth. Then striding ahead of his companion, he confronted our hero.

"Well, you've heard the news I suppose?" he snarled.

"About the announcements being made?" inquired Dick gently.

"No—about me being off the team."

"Yes, I'm sorry, but perhaps——"

"Oh, yes; you're sorry!" snapped Porter. "But I notice that *your* name is down all right."

"Yes," and Dick controlled himself by an effort, for the tone was insulting.

"We all know why you're on the Varsity. It isn't because of your star playing."

"I never claimed to be a star," was the calm answer, "but I probably played well enough to be picked."

"No, you didn't!" fairly shouted Porter. "You were picked because it is your money that's paying the salaries of the coaches and they were afraid if they didn't pick you that they'd lose their jobs. That's why you're on the Varsity, Dick Hamilton, and you can put that in your pipe and smoke it!"

Porter, with a sneer on his puffed and red face, swung around angrily, and started off.

"Wait one minute, Mr. Porter," called Dick in a strangely quiet voice. "I want to say something to you."

"No, let me say it," begged Paul quickly, as Porter turned and faced them.

CHAPTER X

DICK IS REBUFFED

For a moment the four cadets—two on one side and two on the other—stared at each other. The face of Dick Hamilton was rather pale, but he held himself well in control. As for Paul, he had one hand on the shoulder of his chum, and had taken an eager step forward to confront Porter.

That bully regarded the two friends with a sneer on his face, and the countenance of Weston wore an amused smile.

"Well, I thought you were going to say something," half-snarled Porter. "If you are, put some steam on. We're in a hurry."

"You made an accusation just now," went on Paul, making a motion to Dick to keep silent.

"I did, and I think I can back it up. Why it's plain to everybody how the thing is worked. It's even known as Hamilton's football team, and no wonder he is picked to play on it."

"It isn't my team at all!" burst out the young millionaire.

"Well, you're paying for the coaches," put in Weston. "That's why they——"

"They don't know a thing about it!" cried Paul Drew. "That's what I want to say. From the beginning it was feared that something like this might crop up, and so Dick arranged to hand the money to the athletic committee, of which I happen to be a member. Our committee pays the salaries of the coaches, and also for their board, and the coaches themselves only know that much. They have no more idea that Dick is footing the bills than that an inhabitant of Mars is doing it, and if any one makes a statement to the contrary—well, we have a way of dealing with such persons at Kentfield," and Paul looked significantly at Porter and Weston.

"Does that satisfy you?" asked Dick quietly, as Paul paused. "I would have told you the same thing, but perhaps it is just as well to come from a member of the committee. I am only too glad to help out the team by hiring the coaches, but they don't know me from any other player, and I took my chances with all of you. If I had been turned down, as I half expected to be, it would have made no difference."

"Wait until you get turned down, and then you'll sing a different tune," remarked Porter bitterly, and Dick realized how he must feel.

"I'm sorry," said the young millionaire gently, "and if I had any influence at all you should be on the Varsity, for I think you are a good player."

"The coaches don't," and Porter laughed sarcastically.

"There's plenty of chance yet," went on Dick. "We are to have another practice game this week, and there may be a turn about in some players."

"I have a large sized gold framed picture of 'em naming me," exclaimed Porter with sarcasm. "But I take back what I said about your money getting you on. It did seem so, at first."

"Perhaps naturally," agreed Dick. "But your apology is accepted," and he held out his hand. "I hope we can be friends," he concluded.

"I guess so," mumbled Porter, with rather a shamed air.

"I presume Mr. Weston seconds what his friend says," spoke Paul significantly.

"Oh, yes," and it was with rather an obvious effort that the crony made reply. "Come on, Porter, or the best billiard tables will all be occupied."

"Well, I'm glad that's over," remarked Dick to Paul, as they turned away. "I was afraid this would crop up, and it's just as well to settle it. I only hope it does settle it, and that no other fellows will think as Porter and Weston did."

"Oh, some of them are bound to think it anyhow," said Paul easily. "Don't mind it, for it will wear away sooner or later. I'm afraid, though, that the team will be known as yours."

"I don't want that, Paul."

"Can't be helped, old man. After all it's a high honor. I wish I could afford a football team, and a steam yacht."

"Maybe you will some day. And, come to think of it I may not have a steam yacht much longer."

"Why, are you going to sell it?"

"No, but dad's finances are in a bad way, and may become worse."

"You don't mean to say he's lost all his money?" and Paul gave Dick a startled glance.

"Oh, we have enough to keep the wolf from howling under the parlor windows, and I don't expect to have to go to work in Uncle Ezra's woolen mill right away, but dad is involved in some trolley deal, and it's 'crimping' him, as he says. He's got most of his money tied up in it now, and some men, of whom Porter's father is one are trying to get the road away from dad."

"Does Porter know this?"

"He doesn't know it's my father whom his father is fighting, and I'd just as soon he wouldn't. But I've got to do something to help out, and one thing is to locate a Mr. Duncaster," and Dick told of his encounters with the eccentric man, and how he held a large block of stock in the trolley line.

"I'll help if I can," agreed Paul. Then they got their ice cream sodas, and strolled back to the academy.

That night Dick wrote his father a long letter, explaining about the football team, and also detailing his meetings with Mr. Duncaster.

"He lives in a place called Hardvale," wrote Dick, "and he seems to be as hard as the place is named. However, I'll try to see him, and get him to sell you the stock. You had better write me some specific instructions, and say how high I can go in bidding for it. If Mr. Porter, whose son is here at Kentfield, learns that Duncaster has the stock, he may have a try for it, so I'll have to go at it quietly. But I'll do my best."

Then, having done as much as he could in his father's business matters, our hero resumed his interrupted studies.

There was more football practice the next day, and the coaches now put the Varsity team through some rigorous work. The cadets were a little inclined to find fault at the strenuous tasks assigned to them, but the experts were exacting, and said that if Kentfield expected to be in the championship class she must work for it.

Meanwhile the scrub was being moulded into shape, for a good opponent is a necessary element in practice, and unless there is something to fight against practice goes for little.

And how eager that same scrub was to make touchdowns against the Varsity! How they did work, taking desperate chances all the while, and the individual players making names for themselves by brilliant dashes. For they all wanted to get on the first team, and they bore in mind what the coaches had said about giving them a chance if they did well.

"We certainly have our work cut out for us," remarked Dick, after a particularly gruelling day. "I'm as lame as a fellow who's tumbled downstairs."

"Same here," agreed Paul. "Some one walked all over me in that last scrimmage."

But the effect of the hard work was fast becoming noticeable, for the team was getting to be like "nails" as Mr. Martin said, and the players were working more in unison.

There was a practice game between the Varsity and scrub on Saturday, and it was the best one yet, from a critical football viewpoint. The coaches nodded their heads in approval when the first team made six touchdowns. And, though the scrub did manage to get a field goal, it was not to the discredit of the Varsity.

"We're picking up," declared Dick, as he ducked under a shower bath in the gymnasium. "We'll be able to challenge Blue Hill again, and they won't dare turn us down."

"I think we're going to try on some other team first," said Paul. "I heard the coaches talking about it. But say, who's going to be our captain—have you heard?"

"Not a word about it. Maybe it will fall on you, since Teddy is out."

"Jove! it would be an honor, but I don't hope for it. I'd like to see you fill that berth," went on Paul unselfishly.

"Nonsense!" exclaimed Dick. "I guess—blub—glub—ugh!" for he turned his head up and the shower from the spray filled his mouth and nose unexpectedly.

"Wow! That was a wet one!" he cried when he had caught his breath.

"Dutton would like to be captain, I hear," put in George Hall, who was in the next shower to Paul. "He says he's going to try for it."

"And he'd be a good one," declared Dick heartily, for he and his former enemy were now firm friends, though not exactly chums.

There were many speculations as to who would head the eleven, but the coaches had advised the cadets to wait until the Varsity team was definitely selected before holding an election, and this had been agreed to.

There came a long telegram for Dick late that Saturday night. It was from his father, and showed more plainly than anything else how anxious the financier was. For he did not wait to write a reply to Dick's letter, preferring the speed of the wire.

"See Duncaster by all means," read part of the message, "and offer him ten points above par for the stock—all he has. It's a big price, but it will soon be worth more. See him soon."

"I'll make a trip out there Monday," decided Dick. "Whew! Things are beginning to happen evidently."

With Paul for a companion our hero hired an auto and made the journey to Hardvale. Grit sat on the floor of the tonneau, with a contented look on his ugly but honest countenance.

"Grit may come in handy if Duncaster sets his dogs on us," remarked Dick with a grim smile, as they bowled along at good speed.

"Why, do you expect trouble?" asked Paul.

"Not exactly, but I imagine he hasn't much use for me. He didn't act very friendly the last time we met, and then the sight of the auto may make him angry, remembering how we ran him down. But it's too slow to take a horse. I hope we find him at home."

It was rather a lonesome part of the country through which they were traveling—a sparsely settled district that, somehow, reminded the young millionaire of the gloomy landscape at Dankville where his Uncle Ezra lived.

Mr. Duncaster was at home, a fact which a crabbed old housekeeper conveyed to the boys in no very cheerful voice.

"But I don't believe he'll see you," she added. "He's just woke up from his afternoon nap, and he's always a little riled then."

"Hum," mused our hero, "rather an unfavorable time to call, but it can't be helped. Will you tell him Dick Hamilton wants to see him?" he requested of the housekeeper.

"Oh, I s'pose so," and the woman went off grumbling, leaving the two lads standing on the doorstep.

"Polite," commented Paul with a short laugh.

The woman came back presently.

"He wants to know what you want," she said.

"I'd like to see him, and explain in person," said the young millionaire, "but will you tell him it is about the stock of the Midvale Electric Road he holds. I wish to purchase it for my father."

"Oh, you do; eh?" snarled a voice behind the housekeeper, and the wizzened and rather scowling face of Mr. Duncaster was thrust out. "So that's why you called on me, Dick Hamilton? I haven't forgotten you, as you'll note. Ha! There's another of the tin soldiers," he sneered as he caught sight of Paul. "If I had my way you'd all be breaking stone on the road, and you wouldn't have those soldier suits on, either," and he chuckled hoarsely. Clearly he was none the better for his nap.

"I called in reference to the Midvale stock," explained Dick, trying hard to keep down his anger and speak politely. "My father told me to offer you ten above par for it."

"Ten; eh?" and Mr. Duncaster chuckled. "Did he say you were to go higher in case I refused that offer?"

"No, he did not."

"Well then you can go back where you came from and tell your father that I won't sell."

"Do you mean for that price? Do you want more money? I can wire my father, and say——"

"You needn't say anything for me!" snapped the crabbed man. "I won't sell at that price, nor any other he can offer me. I've had a better offer than his, you can tell him, but I won't do business with him. Now get away from here! This isn't war time and I don't want a couple of tin soldiers on my front steps," and once more the old man chuckled at his insulting words.

Dick and Paul flushed, but made no retort.

"Won't you consider any offer at all from my father?" asked the young millionaire, wondering if the other bid for the stock had come from Mr. Porter. "I will send him a message, telling him you——"

"I told you that you needn't tell him anything from me!" snapped Mr. Duncaster. "I won't sell, and that's all there is to it! Now get out!" and he slammed shut the door.

For a moment Dick paused irresolutely on the steps. Then, with a shrug of his shoulders, he said:

"Turned down! Well I'll have to try some other way. It will be a disappointment for dad though."

As the two chums walked out of the yard the chauffeur came toward them with a small pail.

"What are you going to do?" asked Dick.

"Get some water for the radiator. It's almost out. I see a well over here."

He approached it to draw up the bucket, when a window was raised, and the head of Mr. Duncaster was thrust out.

"Here! Keep away from that well!" he cried. "You shan't have any of my water for your old rip-snorting contraption. I believe you are the fellow who ran into me the other night. Get away from there and water your machine somewhere else."

"Hum! You're a cheerful companion for yourself in your old age," remarked the chauffeur, as he turned back.

CHAPTER XI

A RIVALRY

"What are you going to do?" asked Dick of the auto driver, as the three walked out of the yard of the mean man, watched all the way by the squinting eyes of Mr. Duncaster.

"Oh, I'll go to some place down the road where they're not so careful of their water," was the answer.

"Have you enough to run on?" asked Paul, and the chauffeur assured them that he had. The next resident was a cheerful farmer, who not only gave permission for them to take all the water they needed, but even drew it from the well for them.

"And if your machine needs a drink, perhaps you will too," said the farmer's wife. "I've just made some hot coffee, and I'd like you all to come in and have some."

"We will!" assented Dick, and most grateful was the beverage, for riding in the open car was chilly.

"What a difference in people," commented Paul, as they started off again.

The young millionaire felt almost as badly at sending the discouraging news to his father as Mr. Hamilton must have felt on receiving it. But he immediately wired back a cheerful telegram to his son.

"Don't worry," he advised, "we'll try some other way, and perhaps you may be able to get around Duncaster later. I'd come on and tackle him myself, but I can't spare the time."

Thereupon Dick began to devise ways and means of inducing the miserly and crabbed financier to part with the stock. He even thought of taking part of the money that was in his own right, and making an offer higher than the one authorized by his father, but he reflected since Mr. Hamilton had not told him to go more than ten points above par value, perhaps there might be a special reason for this.

"I might take a crowd of the fellows out to his house some night and haze him," ventured our hero.

"Let me go along if you do," begged Paul eagerly. "I'd like to get even with him for calling us tin soldiers."

"I'm afraid it can't be done," and Dick sighed. "I'll have to think of something else."

Football practice now occupied all the spare time the cadets had. Early and late they were on the gridiron, playing under the watchful eyes of the two coaches, who still found many faults to correct.

"No team is perfect," declared Mr. Spencer, "but we want Kentfield to be as nearly so as possible. You boys must do better on kicking though, for you may meet some team where you'll have to depend on your leg-and-foot-work to pull you out of a hole."

"And they're not quite as fast as I'd like to see them," added Mr. Martin. "They don't snap back into place quickly enough after each play. Now try it again. Get in the habit of running back into place instead of walking. Be lively!"

They lined up again, to run through some new plays and formations, and then were ready for the scrub, against whom they made such a good showing that both coaches warmly congratulated their charges.

"I wish poor Teddy was back on the Varsity," confided Dick to Paul, as they finished the day's practice. "He's feeling it very much, and he's falling off in form."

"Yes, I was afraid of that. I wonder if we couldn't do something?"

"I'm afraid not. Porter is playing well on the scrub though. He's much faster than he was in getting down on kicks, and he tackles fiercely. Did you ever have him come at you?"

"Indeed I have," answered Paul ruefully. "I've got a lump on my head yet where he threw me down last week. But that's the way to play the game."

"Sure. Say, don't you think it's rather queer not to have a captain?"

"Yes, and it's evident that Teddy isn't going to stand any show for it now. It will be some one of the present team, I fancy."

"Probably. Have you heard any rumors?"

"Well, George Hall would like it—in fact every fellow would, but Dutton is the hottest after it. He's pulling wires all he can—in a legitimate way, of course, and lots of the fellows like him."

"I don't blame him. Well, I'll vote for him, when the election is held."

"I won't!" declared Paul stoutly.

"Why not?"

"Because I'm going to vote for you, old man."

"Nonsense! I don't know as I want it."

"You deserve it, which is more. No one has done as much for the Kentfield eleven since the academy was started as you have this one season, and you ought to be captain. Then you couldn't kick when they called it Dick Hamilton's football team."

"Oh, get out!" cried the young millionaire, yet he was not displeased at his chum's sincere words. And what normal healthy lad would not want to be captain of an eleven?

There was much buzzing talk the next few days concerning the captaincy, and when the coaches announced that the present Varsity eleven would stand, at least for the present, and that in order to play match games a captain would be needed, the excitement grew apace.

"Nominations to-morrow night!" cried Paul one afternoon as he burst into the room he and Dick shared. "Dutton's name is sure to go up. I'm going to nominate you and I've got the promise of nearly enough votes to put you through."

"Look here!" began Dick, "I don't want——"

"It doesn't matter what you want!" cried Paul, clapping his chum on the back, and doing a sort of war dance around him, "you haven't anything to say in this matter. You just come to the meeting and see what happens."

It was a lively session, for several matters cropped up that needed to be settled. There was also a manager to be chosen, and, as Beeby did not want the place, preferring to spend more time in practice and training, it was practically decided to have some one not on the team to look after business ends.

Dan Hatfield was talked of for manager, and his name met with such instant favor that none other was considered. But when it came to the captaincy that was a different matter.

The little boom that started in favor of George Hall was so feeble that he himself saw that he had no chance, and nipped it. There was much talking and putting together of heads when Mr. Martin arose to announce that nominations for captain were in order, and that the names would be posted three days, and then voted on.

"I nominate Ray Dutton!" sung out John Stiver, who was the particular chum of the former.

It was quickly seconded, and then up jumped Paul Drew.

"I nominate Dick Hamilton!" he sung out.

"Second it!" came promptly from Dutton himself, a courtesy that Dick acknowledged with a bow.

The former rivals—now rivals again—faced each other with smiles, but there were anxious feelings in the hearts of both.

"Three cheers for the candidates!" cried Jim Watkins, and they were given heartily, with a tiger added.

"Any more nominations?" asked Mr. Martin.

"Well there's luck in odd numbers, I nominate Frank Rutley!" called out Porter with a laugh. "We might as well have a good choice while we're at it."

Weston seconded this name, and there were no comments. Thereupon the three names were posted on the bulletin board, and the meeting adjourned.

"Well, what do you think of it, Dick?" asked Paul, as they strolled back to their room.

"I'm glad I'm nominated, of course, but——"

"Well, but me no buts, what is it?"

"Dutton is very popular, and I can't help remembering how he was against me when I first came here. But I'll take my chance with him!"

CHAPTER XII

THE MIDNIGHT ALARM

Wire-pulling extraordinary went on at Kentfield for the next two days. Each candidate had his particular friends, who worked hard to gain votes for him.

It was soon seen that Rutley had no chance, and though he would poll several votes, the main contest was between Dutton and Dick Hamilton.

"And you're going to win!" declared Paul with enthusiasm, as he clapped his chum on the back. "I've got nearly enough votes promised right now, and I know I can gain over more of the fellows."

"But say, old man, don't make such a fuss. You make me feel——"

"No matter how you feel, you're going to be captain! I'm sure of it!"

"Well, there's no use saying I don't care how the election goes, for I do," declared Dick honestly. "I'd rather it was some one else than Dutton though, who was against me."

"Why, you're not afraid of him; are you?"

"No, but you remember the old rivalry. I'm afraid it will make talk, but I want to say right here and now that if he is elected he won't have any better friend than I, and I'll play my head off to help his team win!"

"We all know that!" cried Paul, looking at his chum admiringly. "It goes without saying. Now I'm off to see some more of the first year fellows."

"Don't make too much of a fuss about it," begged Dick. "Don't make it look as though I'd give my head to be elected. I want it, of course, but——"

"I understand!" cried Paul lightly as he hurried off.

As the time for election drew nearer the excitement increased and there were all sorts of rumors floating around. Votes were openly bought and sold, but in a friendly, boyish fashion, the inducements being nothing more important than "treats" or some special favors. Some even traded the horses assigned to them in the cavalry drills, one cadet getting a handsome black he coveted in exchange for a rather poor roan, but Dick gained a vote thereby.

Paul Drew was a faithful lieutenant in his chum's cause, and he did valiant work. As for the young millionaire and Dutton, they kept discreetly out of it. They met several times during the course of the first day's electioneering, and gaily chaffed each other on the chances they stood.

"I hear you won't have one vote, 'Ham,'" laughingly declared Dick's former enemy.

"That's right," half-seriously assented our hero. "I told all my friends to vote for you."

"So I heard. Kind of you. Come on over and I'll buy you a soda."

"No. They're on the forbidden training menu now."

"That's so, I nearly forgot. Well, come on up to the Sacred Pig, and we'll have some toast and tea," for there was a lunch room in the society house. The two rivals went off arm in arm, watched by an admiring throng of cadets, for they were both great favorites with their schoolmates.

At the close of the first day it was generally admitted by the workers on both sides that the two candidates for captain had about the same number of votes. Rutley was "not in it," as Paul said, and the lad himself laughingly admitted this. Still Porter and his particular set were working in his interests, not so much because they really wanted him, as that they did not want Dick to win, and they took this means of deflecting votes from him. At the last minute, it was rumored, the Rutley votes would be swung to Dutton.

"But you've got heaps of chances yet, Dick," declared Paul, "and there's lots more time to canvass."

But not much electioneering could be done on the next day, for a competitive drill was ordered and after that was to come artillery practice. There was barely a chance for some football work, and it had to be cut short.

What little was done, however, demonstrated that the team was shaping up well, and the coaches were more than pleased.

"We'll have them play the Dunkirk Military Academy next Saturday," announced Mr. Spencer, "and we'll see what they can do in a real contest."

"I have great hopes of them," declared Mr. Martin. "Of course they ought to beat Dunkirk, for it's a smaller academy than this, but if they roll up a big score, bigger than Blue Hill did against the same team last year, Blue Hill can hardly refuse to play our boys, and I understand that their refusal to meet Kentfield is a sore point."

"It certainly is. Oh, we'll whip our lads into shape yet, and then Blue Hill can look to her laurels."

The two coaches walked over to the gymnasium, for they kept themselves in condition by hard physical work on the apparatus, as well as by out-door practice.

All through the academy that night went the buzz and hum of talk about the election. Several votes changed hands, so to speak, though it could not be said that Dick's chances were increased thereby. In fact Paul was a little downcast as he reckoned up the number he was sure of for his chum, and thought of the number needed.

"But I'll get them!" he told himself fiercely as he looked at the list in his hand. "There are some new fellows I haven't seen yet."

"Oh, go to bed," advised Dick, who was tired with the day's duties, but Paul would not.

The young millionaire was sleeping soundly when Paul came in a little later.

"Well?" asked Dick, half awake.

"Not very well," answered Paul dubiously, "but it may be in the morning. Dutton certainly has lots of friends."

"All right," announced Dick as cheerfully as he could.

It was after midnight when the two chums, as well as several other cadets, were awakened by an alarm wildly shouted.

"Fire! Fire! Fire!" came in startled tones from a voice they recognized as that of Toots. "Fire in the ammunition house!"

Paul and Dick were out of bed in the same instant, and rushed to the window. They saw a red glare, and the cry of Toots was echoed by other janitors.

"By Jove! The ammunition house is blazing!" cried Paul aghast. "If that goes up——"

"It's far enough removed from the main buildings," cried Dick, as he began hurriedly to dress, "but it may damage the Sacred Pig. Besides, there are some valuable guns in there—and Paul—I forgot—Grit is in there! Come on!" and Dick raced from the room, half attired as he was.

CHAPTER XIII

THE RESCUE OF DUTTON

"What do you mean? Grit in there—in the ammunition house?" cried Paul, hurrying after his chum. He wondered whether he had understood Dick rightly.

"Yes, he's there," came the reply, and the young millionaire never turned around as he sped down the corridor that was rapidly filling with half-dressed cadets who had been aroused by the cries of the janitors. "They're repairing the stable where I keep him nights, and as it was unlocked I put Grit in the powder house so no one would steal him. Now it's on fire!"

"We'll get him!" cried Paul. "Come on, fellows, Dick's dog is in there!"

The flames were now more plainly visible, and they were gaining rapidly. Two of the janitors, one of whom was Toots, had pails of water and were dashing the fluid on the fire, while others were unreeling a hose.

The ammunition house was a large one, made in the main of concrete, but there was built on it a small, wooden shed under which some empty packing boxes and cases were stored, and where some garden tools were kept. It was this shed which had caught fire, and unless it was quickly put out the flames might communicate to the wooden door of the powder house proper. There could be but one result then—an explosion.

Everyone realized this as he rushed on to fight the fire. Some of the professors were now up and were issuing orders, but there was so much excitement that no one paid much attention to them.

"Is there a good water pressure?" panted Paul.

"I don't know," answered Dick, as he ran on. "There was the other day when we had fire drill, but maybe just when we want it there won't be any."

"Hurry! Hurry!" shouted Toots, as he and the others dashed pail after pail of water on the fire.

"Use the hose! Turn on the water!" cried Ray Dutton, who was just ahead of Dick. "Why don't you turn on the pressure?"

"Guess they don't know how to do it," answered the young millionaire. "One of those men is a new hand. Come on, boys, I can't see Grit burned to death!"

"He's howling now," cried Paul.

Indeed the frightened yelping of the imprisoned animal could be heard above the roar and crackle of the flames, and Dick increased his speed.

"I'm coming, Grit! I'm coming!" he shouted, but it is doubtful if the dog heard him.

The burning shed was in front of the only door to the ammunition house, and the fire must first be extinguished before the portal could be reached. To go through the flames now was out of the question.

"Keep back, boys! Keep back!" cried Major Webster. "There may be an explosion any moment. Keep back!"

"But my dog is in there!" shouted Dick. "I must get Grit out!"

"You can't. It's madness to go too close!"

"I'm going to!" replied Dick grimly. "We'll put out the fire."

"Then use the hose—don't go too close with the buckets. That wooden shed should never have been built where it is."

"Come on! Get the hose into action!" yelled Dutton, and taking the nozzle from the hands of puzzled and inexperienced men, the cadet directed it at the fire, while Dick and Paul, aided by some of their companions, turned on the water, the supply coming from a big storage tank, raised high on metal supports to give the necessary force.

A moment later the water spurted from the nozzle and sprayed on the fire with a hiss of steam.

"That's the stuff!" shouted Dick. "We'll soon have you out of there, Grit! Wait a minute, old boy!"

This time the dog heard his master's voice, and a joyful bark replaced his howls of fear.

It was high time that there be used some more effective means of putting out the fire than buckets of water, for the flames were burning fiercely.

"It's lucky that the door of the powder house is thick," murmured Major Webster. "It will take some time to burn through. But if it does——"

He did not finish his half-spoken thought, but shuddered as he looked at the cadets grouped around the burning structure. He wanted to order them away, but he knew the only safety lay in putting out the flames to prevent the explosion. And the cadets seemed to be the only ones capable of handling the situation, for the janitors had completely lost their heads and were so confused that they could not obey the simplest order.

"Get the other hose into action!" cried the major, for there were two small lines available for use at the powder house. "You'll never get it out with one."

"I'll attend to it!" answered Dick, and, leaving Dutton and Paul to manage the one line, he and John Stiver ran to the other and began unreeling that.

The flames were now at their height, and were blazing high, the loose and light wood of the packing boxes making excellent fuel.

"Hurry! Hurry!" nervously ordered the major, doing all he could. Colonel Masterly and some of the other instructors now arrived, but there was little they could do.

"If we can only keep the fire away from the door a little longer," murmured the colonel. "They are subduing it, don't you think, Major?"

"They are doing good work—plucky lads. It takes an emergency like this to show their mettle."

"Do you think the door will catch?"

"I hope not, but——"

It was a vain hope, as they could see a moment later.

A puff of wind blew the smoke and flames aside for a second, and the two men could look plainly at the thick door of the ammunition building. What they saw caused them to start back, for a tiny whisp of fire was eating away at the edge of the portal.

"Too late!" groaned the colonel. "We must get the boys back! We shall have to let it burn. Get back, boys! Get back!"

"We'll have it out in another minute!" yelled Dick, as he turned on the water from his line. "I'm going to save Grit!"

The fire died down for a few seconds, owing to the increased amount of water poured on it, but it was only for a moment, and then it flared up again. But the cadets fought on grimly. Some were even using pails, dipping water from a nearby cistern, and they would not obey the orders of the teachers to keep back. They did little good, however, as they could not get near enough to make much of the fluid effective.

The door of the powder house was now burning in a larger area, and it seemed that the explosion might come at any moment. All saw it, and while they knew that they themselves could get a safe distance away, and while they realized that even if the powder did blow up, none of the college buildings would be damaged, it was different in the case of their favorite club house—the Sacred Pig—for it was close to the blazing structure.

"It will be 'roast pig' in a few minutes," murmured Paul Drew ruefully.

"I should say yes," agreed Dutton. "But we won't let it happen. If only the water holds out!"

Once more came a howl from the imprisoned Grit.

"Poor dog!" cried Dick, stooping down to see if there was a chance to get in and save his pet. But there seemed to be none.

Almost at that instant the roof of the burning shed fell in, carrying with it part of the half consumed structure. This gave a better view of the powder house door, which was seen to be on fire in several places. Grit's howls of anguish became louder.

"I can't stand that—I'm going to save him!" cried Dutton to George Hall.

"But how can you? You can't get near the place."

"Yes, I can—there's a side window. I wonder some of us didn't think of it before. I can reach it by a short ladder, and break open the window with an axe. Here goes. You handle the hose in my place."

Before George could make any objection, Dutton had thrust the nozzle into his friend's hand and was running toward the powder house. On his way he caught up a light ladder and a fire axe that was on one of the hose reel carts.

"Where are you going, Dutton?" called Major Webster.

"To get Dick's dog—out through the window. I can do it all right."

"Come back!" cried the major, but the cadet did not heed.

Dick was having his hands full with the hose and for a moment he did not see what his former enemy had done. The fire was a little less fierce now, as the material on which it fed had been nearly all consumed, but the door was blazing in spots. They played water on it, but as fast as one area of fire was extinguished it would break out in another.

There came a crash of glass and a cry from Dutton.

"I'm in! Look out for Grit. Here he comes—through the window!"

"Grit! Through the window!" cried Dick in amazement. "Why—how——?"

"Ray went in after him!" called George Hall.

"There's the dog."

At that instant the cadet inside the powder house thrust Grit out of the window. The brute fell harmlessly in a heap on the grass, but sprang up a moment later and rushed toward the fire-fighting cadets.

"Here, old man!" cried Dick, and the dog went into a demonstration of joy, fawning all over his master, while the youth hugged the ugly but loving animal close in his arms, the hose being grasped by ready hands as he let go of it.

"Come out, Dutton, come out!" cried Major Webster. "Come out at once."

Hardly had he spoken than there sounded from within the powder house a dull explosion. It was not a hard one, and no evidences of it could be observed outside the structure. But the cadets and professors looked at each other in alarm, their faces lighted up by the dancing flames. They all knew what it meant.

"The beginning of the end!" remarked the colonel gravely. "Get back, everyone! I order it!"

"But Ray Dutton is in there!" cried Dick. "He may be injured and can't get out. I'm going to save him!"

The young millionaire sprang away. Grit started to follow.

"Come back at once!" ordered the colonel.

"Not until I save him!" answered Dick. "He risked his life to save my dog, and now I'll rescue him! Go back, Grit. Wait for me."

The dog whined but obeyed, and Dick ran on. As he passed by the second hose reel he grasped from it an axe. Straight for the door of the powder house he ran, the water from the two lines of hose falling in a spray around him.

The fire was now sufficiently out to permit of reaching the portal over the wet embers which still glowed faintly. The shed had fallen apart and what was left of it was burning on one side. Little tongues of flame spurted here and there on the main door.

Dick rushed up and with the axe began raining blows on the portal. His fellow cadets cheered lustily, and then devoted all their energies to keeping the water playing about their brave comrade. He was soaked through but in this lay his only safety, for the flames still were dangerously close.

There came another slight explosion inside the powder house. Evidently small cases of the gun cartridges were going off, but as they were all blanks there was no danger from bullets.

"Ray—are you alive—are you all right?" cried Dick, as he paused for a moment. There was no answer, and he rained the blows from the axe more madly than before.

With a crash the door gave way. Flinging his implement aside, Dick sprang into the powder house. There was an anxious moment, and the cadets and instructors waited in fear and trembling.

"He may be overcome by the powder fumes," said the colonel. "Poor lads—they may both be killed."

An instant after the colonel had spoken a form appeared in the blackened doorway. One form? No, two, for in his arms Dick Hamilton bore the limp body of Dutton.

"He's got him! He's got him!" yelled Paul Drew, and a great shout followed his words.

On staggered Dick with his burden. Grit saw his master in the now dimming light from the fire, and barked joyfully.

"Back! Get back everybody!" panted the young millionaire. "She's going up! There's a fire inside! Get back—quick!"

CHAPTER XIV

THE ELECTION

Dick was seen to stagger, and it was no wonder, for Ray Dutton was no light weight.

"Let me help you!" shouted Paul, as he ran toward his chum. He grasped the limp legs of the unconscious cadet, while Dick carried the shoulders, and together they hastened on.

"Back! Get back!" cried Dick again, as his schoolmates crowded up around him and Paul. "The explosion will come any minute! There's fire in there!"

"Back this instant, every one of you! You can't do anything more!" cried Colonel Masterly sternly, and the boys knew it was now time to obey. Those holding the hose lines dropped them, and the crowd of fire-fighters surged back.

"Is Dutton dead?" gasped Paul.

"Not dead—and not hurt much, I hope," answered Dick. "He was overcome by the powder fumes—there was a little explosion almost as soon as he got inside—some sparks must have blown in the window. But he saved Grit."

"And you saved him."

"Come on, we'd better get farther back!" cried the young millionaire as Paul hesitated, and was about to lay Dutton down. "The force of it will——"

His voice was drowned in a detonating report, and the darkness of the night was lighted by an intense glare. The powder house had blown up, and the wind of the concussion knocked down Paul and Dick in a heap with the unconscious Dutton. Other cadets who had not run far enough back were also bowled over.

Then came intense blackness, following the bright flash and this was succeeded by the patter of small missiles tossed into the air by the force of the powder.

"Jove, I hope none of the chunks of concrete come this way!" cried Paul as he got up. "Are you hurt, Dick?"

"Not a bit of it. Look at Dutton though."

"He doesn't seem to be," answered Paul, as he looked at the unconscious cadet as well as he could in the dim light that came from a few scattered and burning embers blown here and there by the explosion.

"Oh—I'm—I'm all right," gasped Dutton, as he slowly sat up. "What happened?"

"My it sounds good to hear you speak again!" cried Dick, as he put his arms around his friend and assisted him to arise. "You were overcome in there when you went in to get Grit, and I took you out. Now the whole thing has gone up, but it doesn't seem to have done much damage."

Scores of cadets now crowded around the three lads. The rain of missiles had ceased, and quick inquiries showed that beyond a few scratches or bruises no one was seriously hurt. The heavy concrete side of the walls of the powder house had merely toppled outward, almost in four solid pieces, and it was only the light wooden roof, purposely made so, that had been much shattered. It was the fragments of this that had rained down.

The fire was effectually scattered by the explosion and what little remained was quickly extinguished by the janitors with pails of water, and one hose line. The other had been blown apart and was useless.

Colonel Masterly and the other instructors went about among the lads, making sure that none needed hospital treatment. They came to where Dick, Paul and Ray stood.

"Hamilton, let me congratulate you on your pluck and daring in saving your comrade's life," said the colonel gravely, as he shook hands with Dick in the light of several lanterns that had been brought up. "It was a brave act."

"Well, he saved Grit, and it was the only way I could pay him back," replied our hero simply, as he fondled the dog that leaped up on him with demonstrative affection.

"I couldn't bear to hear Grit howl," explained Ray, who had now recovered from the powder fumes. "Let's go see if the Sacred Pig is much damaged," he added quickly, for neither he nor Dick liked to pose as heroes.

"I fancy the building is not much harmed," spoke the colonel. "Most of the force of the explosion was upward. You young gentlemen deserve a vote of thanks from the faculty for the manner in which you acquitted yourselves to-night, and I will see that you get it. Now we had better go back to the dormitories. The night is rather chilly." Indeed it was, lightly clad as everyone was.

Beyond a few shattered windows, and some broken glassware in the pantry, the society house of the Sacred Pig was not damaged, at which the cadets were very glad. The excitement quieted down, and after the doctor had looked over Dutton, and pronounced him safe and sound, the students went back to their beds, but hardly to sleep much.

An investigation was made the next day, to discover if possible the cause of the fire, but beyond the fact that it had started in some refuse of the shed nothing could be learned.

"It was careless on my part to allow the shed to be there," said the colonel. "When we rebuild the ammunition house I will have it placed farther off, and there will be no wooden structures attached to it. We must not risk another accident like this."

In view of the fire, lessons were suspended that day, and only a short drill ordered. When this was over the electioneering began again, for in the afternoon the selection of the football captain was to be made.

There was quite a change of sentiment, and Paul Drew found that he had to do very little pleading now to get the promise of votes for Dick.

"It was the pluckiest and nerviest thing I ever saw done," declared Harvey Nolan, one of the new cadets, who had hitherto resisted Paul's pleadings, being firm for Dutton. "I like Ray immensely, but I think I'll vote for Hamilton."

"If this keeps on it will be unanimous for him," said Paul in delight. He was hardly prepared for what followed.

The cadets were assembled in the gymnasium, and Mr. Martin, by request, was presiding over the important session.

"I understand you are now ready to proceed with the election for a captain and a manager," began the Yale coach.

"Sure," came the inelegant but hearty reply from several.

"There are three candidates," went on the coach. "Mr. Hamilton, Mr. Dutton and Mr. Rutley. How will you vote, by ballot or acclimation?"

"Ballot—ballot!" came the cry.

"Very well, then I will appoint the tellers, and you——"

"One moment, if you please," interrupted Dutton, as he arose. "There has been a slight mistake made. There are only two candidates in the field—Mr. Hamilton and Mr. Rutley. I wish to withdraw in favor of Mr. Hamilton. You—you all know what he did last night—for me," faltered Ray, and his voice was a trifle husky. "After that I could not stand against him in the election."

"Yes, you will—I insist!" cried Dick, jumping up. "I don't want you to withdraw."

"You can't help yourself, old man!" cried Ray heartily, playfully shaking his fist at Dick. "I want all you fellows who were going to vote for me to vote for Dick Hamilton—that is unless you are committed to Frank Rutley," and he bowed in the direction of that cadet.

"No one can vote for me—I'm out of it!" called out Frank. "I'm for Hamilton."

"Hurray!" cried Paul Drew.

"Three cheers for Dick Hamilton!" sung out someone, and how those cheers were given!

"Do I understand that both you young gentlemen withdraw?" asked Mr. Martin.

"I do," answered Ray.

"Same here!" called Frank.

"Then, as there is but one candidate in the field, perhaps it is unnecessary——"

"I move that Dick Hamilton be unanimously elected captain of the Kentfield football eleven, by acclamation, and long may he wave o'er the team of the strong and the team of the brave!" cried Dutton.

"Second it!" cried Frank.

"All those in favor of this motion will signify it by saying 'yes,'" called the coach.

"YES!" was the reverbrating shout that fairly made the walls ring.

"Then Dick Hamilton is the football captain, and I beg to extend him my congratulations," said Mr. Martin.

"And I, also," added his colleague, and the two coaches stepped from the platform, and advanced toward the blushing young millionaire, while his friends crowded around him to do him honor.

CHAPTER XV

THE GAME WITH DUNKIRK

There was little else to do at the meeting in the way of business. Dan Hatfield was unanimously named for manager, and then the coaches announced that after a few more days of practice the team would be ready for the first game of the season, to be played on the grounds of the Dunkirk Military Academy, a school similar to that of Kentfield, and situated about twenty miles away.

"It is rather a disadvantage not to open on your own grounds," said Mr. Spencer, "but it cannot be helped. I hope you will play all the better for the slight handicap, and I am sure you can win if you try."

"Yes, Dunkirk is hardly in your class," put in Mr. Martin, "but it was the best arrangement we could make under the circumstances. You really need practice against other opponents than your own scrub eleven, and this will give it to you. If you roll up a good big score, then it will be time to talk of taking on Blue Hill, and some of the larger teams."

"Blue Hill beat Dunkirk twenty-six to nothing last year," remarked Dick.

"Then you want to take their measure about forty-six to nothing," remarked Mr. Martin, "and I trust you do it."

There was some hard practice in the next few days, harder practice than any the cadets had yet experienced, but the effects of it were noticeable. They had more confidence in themselves, they were better kickers, quicker in getting down the field, and in offensive work they played together like clockwork. On the defense there was still something to be desired, but that would come with practice the coaches knew.

"Well I guess I'd better go to the railroad station and arrange about getting the tickets for the team to go to Dunkirk to-morrow," remarked Manager Hatfield, the day before the game.

"You needn't get any tickets for the team and substitutes," spoke Dick.

"Why not?"

"Because I've hired some touring automobiles that will take us over and bring us back."

"You have! Say, Hamilton, there's class to you all right! You're a brick! This will be great, and we'll save the money in the treasury. We need it, too. I hope we get a good crowd to swell the gate receipts."

The team that was to open the season was the same that had been practicing against the scrub lately. Teddy Naylor could not make good, and so was not to play, but he was promised by the coaches that he would be the first substitute called on, and this was some consolation. Porter was warned that unless he trained and practiced better he would be dropped altogether, and his sullen answer was that he "didn't much care."

As many of the Kentfield cadets as could manage it went on the train to see the game. Four big cars, which Dick generously hired, transported the team and substitutes, and they started off amid cheers and songs, with the auto gaily decorated with flags.

"It's a good start all right," remarked Paul to Dick, as they flew down the road.

"Yes, and I hope the coming back will be even better."

"Why, you're not afraid of not beating them; are you?"

"Not exactly afraid, but I never was captain of a big football eleven before, and I guess I'm a bit nervous. Of course we'll beat Dunkirk, but I want it to be by a big score."

"Oh, don't worry. We'll make out all right."

There was a big crowd in the grandstands when the team and substitutes drove up, and they were received with cheers as they alighted from the autos. The Dunkirk team had not yet appeared, but their manager met Hatfield, was introduced to Dick, and then the lads were escorted to their dressing rooms.

"There come our fellows," remarked Dutton a little later when, as he was slipping into his jersey, a great cheer was heard, followed by the Kentfield cry.

"Yes, and they've got their voices with them," said Dick. "They're great shouters."

When the Kentfield team trotted out they were met with a rousing welcome of vocal sounds, not only from their own cohorts, but from the Dunkirk sympathizers.

"They're friendly all right," remarked Dick. "Come on, fellows, we'll line up and run through some signals."

He and his men were soon in practice, and the young captain was glad to note that no one had gone stale. Everyone seemed on the alert.

A little later the Dunkirk team trotted out, to be met with a salvo of cheers, and then they, too, lined up and began to work with the ball.

"They are a fast, snappy, little lot, but I think we have them for weight," remarked Paul, looking critically at their opponents.

Dunkirk won the toss, and elected to defend the north goal. Kentfield was to kick off, and on the whole Dick was rather glad, as he could thus early get the measure of the offensive tactics of their enemies.

Beeby sent the ball spinning well down the field as the echoes of the whistle died away. The pigskin was neatly caught, and one of the Dunkirk players began running back with it.

"Nail him, fellows," cried Dick. "Don't let him gain much!" George Hall broke through the interference and had the man down before he had covered ten yards. Then came the line up.

"Watch out now, boys," warned the captain, as the Dunkirk quarter-back began giving the signal.

At the line of Kentfield came a man, hurling himself toward a hole that had been partly opened between Paul Drew and George Hall. Into the opening the man went, but no further, for he was neatly stopped. Only a yard was gained.

"That's the way to do it!" cried Dick in delight. "Hold 'em, boys! Hold 'em!"

Once more Dunkirk made a gallant try, this time around left end, but again the man with the ball was nailed, and thrown for a loss.

"They'll have to kick," cried Dick. "Watch out!"

The backs retreated, and it was well they did for Dunkirk had a powerful ball-booster in the shape of their full-back, and the leather went well into the territory of our friends.

Hal Foster caught it, and protected by excellent interference he rushed it well back before he was downed.

"Now to see what we can do!" exclaimed Dick, as he knelt down back of Jim Watkins, to pass the ball. He signalled for Frank Rutley to take the ball through right tackle, and it was executed to perfection. In vain did the Dunkirk captain beg and plead with his men to hold. Dick's players pushed and shoved Frank through for a ten yard gain.

"That's going some!" panted the left tackle as he took his place again.

Dunkirk was saddened by the advance, thus easily made, though she was not discouraged. But when Ray Dutton went through the line for another substantial gain, and when, without the necessity for kicking in the next scrimmage, John Stiver got through between tackle and guard for eight yards, then there were anxious hearts.

"Walk up for a touchdown!" called several in the crowd of Kentfield supporters in the grand stand.

"We'll do it!" cried Dick.

The coveted touchdown came a few minutes later, the ball having been carried down the field in a series of whirlwind rushes. Paul Drew was shoved over the line, and then Jim Watkins kicked goal.

"Our first points!" cried Dick in delight. "Now the team is beginning to play."

And play they did. It was a foregone conclusion after that, and Dunkirk had no chance. They realized it, and when, after the first half, there were thirty points in favor of Kentfield, and none for their opponents, the captain of Dunkirk said to Dick:

"Our only hope now is to hold you down. You're better off now than Blue Hill was against us."

"That's what we're after," declared the young millionaire. "We're going to wallop Blue Hill when we get the chance, too."

The second half was a repetition of the first. Once on a fumble Dunkirk got the ball, and another time as a penalty for holding on the part of too eager George Hall. The home team tried desperately hard to score, and several of their men were knocked out, but it was not to be.

Once, when because of a miscalculation, the man with the ball got through Dick's line, the young captain had a momentary fear lest his team be scored against. But Hal Foster was on the alert and nailed the panting man with the ball.

There came some fierce scrimmages for Dunkirk was desperate, and Hal was knocked out. This gave Teddy Naylor a chance to get in the game, and he rushed in with eager impetuosity.

"I'm going to make a touchdown!" he declared. "Let me try, Dick."

He was given a chance, and made good, bursting through the line of Dunkirk players, shaking off a fierce tackle by the full-back, and making a score after a forty yard run amid frantic cheers.

After that the Kentfield lads took it a little easier, for which their opponents were duly grateful. Teddy Naylor kicked a beautiful field goal, and then time was called, with the score fifty to nothing in favor of "Dick Hamilton's team," as his chums insisted on calling it.

"Oh, but I feel good!" cried our hero as he ran to the dressing rooms.

"You look like a peach," said Paul. "One eye is half closed and your nose looks as if some one had hammered brass work on it."

"They did, I guess. But you're no picture either. Look at your left ear."

"Wish I could. But never mind. We beat 'em!"

CHAPTER XVI

A DARING PLAN

"Well, what do you boys think of yourselves?" asked Coach Martin the day after the game with Dunkirk, when the football eleven and its supporters had gathered in the gymnasium preparatory to going out to practice.

"Why, did we do so rotten?" asked Innis.

"Had we ought to have piled up a bigger score?" inquired George Hall.

"We did make a few fumbles—at least I did, and once I didn't take care of my man," admitted Jim Watkins. "But——"

"No, I haven't a bit of fault to find," went on Mr. Martin. "I was just wondering whether you felt more confident of your playing ability than you did before we came. I want to get a sort of line on my ability."

"Yes," put in Mr. Spencer, "we are far from finding fault with you, for, on the contrary I think you did exceptionally well. We couldn't ask for any better results, but what Mr. Martin means is whether or not you yourselves feel satisfied."

There was a moment's hesitation. The boys did not know exactly how to take the questions.

"I wish we could beat Blue Hill to a standstill," murmured Captain Dick.

"And then wallop Mooretown," added Ray Dutton.

"Say, can't we challenge Blue Hill now?" asked John Stiver eagerly.

"Yes, let's do it!" came a chorus of voices.

"Better wait," advised Mr. Martin with a laugh and a quick look at his colleague. "If you sent Blue Hill another challenge so soon, they'd only laugh at you, and very likely they would say you arranged the whole coaching plan merely to beat them. If you will permit us to suggest something, we have another scheme."

"What is it?" sung out Innis with engaging frankness.

"We will play some other strong team before we again ask Blue Hill to let us have a chance at them," suggested Mr. Martin. "Then, if we win, as I hope we shall, we will be more in their class. Beating Dunkirk hardly put us there, even though we made a bigger score against them than Blue Hill did. And then, after you get your second wind, so to speak, we will consider getting into the Military League. Do you agree to that plan?"

"Sure!" came instantly from all present. The boys would have agreed to anything that would have paved the way to tackling Blue Hill.

"Then we'll go ahead on that understanding," proceeded the coach. "And now for the second part of the plan. You know it is of little benefit to play some team weaker than you are. What you want to do is to take on some eleven that you know is going to be hard to beat. That will bring out whatever good points we have not yet discovered. Is that clear?"

Once more the boys looked at each other in some astonishment. What was the coach leading to?

"Am I making myself clear?" he asked again.

"Yes. Sure. Go ahead," were some of the answers.

"Then the plan of Mr. Spencer and myself is this," went on Mr. Martin. "We will put you through some hard practice in the next week, and then we will challenge Haskell University."

For a moment there was a period of intense silence in the room. Then several half-astonished gasps could be heard. Once more the boys looked at one another, but this time, instead of with puzzled glances, it was more with looks of fear, or at least uncertainty.

"Haskell University," murmured Dick Hamilton.

"Champions of the Military League year before last," added Innis.

"And likely to be again this year," put in George Hall.

"And he wants us to tackle them—us the tail-enders," muttered Jim Watkins. "It can't be did! We'd all be in the hospital, fellows, and our team would be crippled."

Talk was flying thick and fast now, and almost every remark seemed to be against the daring plan of the coaches. Then Dick realized that he, as captain, ought to say something. It would not do to knuckle under in this craven fashion. A team to do anything must do or dare.

"If Haskell will take us on, we'll play them," he said simply, as he arose in his seat. "But will they, after Blue Hill turned us down?"

"I'm glad that at least your captain isn't afraid," spoke Mr. Spencer, for he and his colleague had heard the half-suppressed whispers of objection. "I know it sounds like a big thing to you, for I know what a strong team Haskell has. But I believe it will do you good to play that eleven. Of course if you don't feel that you could stand the pace, or——"

"Go on! Challenge 'em! We'll play 'em."

"Of course we will."

"And beat 'em, too!"

These expressions took the place of those heard a few minutes before. It argued a good change of heart.

"I'm glad to hear that," commented Mr. Martin. "Then if Manager Hatfield will confer with us after the meeting and practice, we will arrange to get a date with them."

"But will they play us?" asked Dick. "You know they always like to arrange big games, and they may not want to take us on."

"Oh, I fancy that can be arranged," spoke Mr. Martin easily. "Mr. Spencer and I know the coach there and he is a good friend of ours. I am acquainted with the captain, too, and I am almost sure they will give us a game. Now let me congratulate you once more on the showing you made yesterday, and suggest that we get out to practice. We can't get any too much if we are to play Haskell—and beat them." He concluded his remarks with a grim smile.

"Beat 'em! We'll be lucky if we hold 'em down to as much as the score by which we beat Dunkirk," remarked George Hall, as he stepped out beside Captain Dick.

"Here! None of that!" cried the young millionaire, half seriously.

"None of what?" asked George.

"That treason talk," replied Dick. "I want you all to feel that we're going to win, or there isn't much use playing."

"Oh, well, just as you say," agreed George with a laugh. "Do you think we'll win, Paul Drew?"

"Of course," was the answer, for Paul was always loyal to his chum.

As several of the cadets were lame and stiff from the unusual exertion in the Dunkirk game, only light practice was indulged in. Several minor faults were corrected, and then the coaches put their charges through some wing-shift plays, and gave them a chance to improve their work in the on-side kick and the forward pass, in both of which the Kentfield lads were a trifle uncertain.

"Oh, we'll have you in shape to tackle Haskell before you know it," said Mr. Martin encouragingly.

If any of the players were doubtful about this they did not say so, and they took heart from the confident air Dick Hamilton assumed.

In the days that followed the practice gradually became more and more rigorous, and, as a result, fast, snappy playing became the order of the day.

"Have you heard whether or not Haskell will play us?" asked Paul of Dick one night, as they sat in their room studying and waiting for "taps" to sound.

"No, I haven't. I meant to ask Hatfield to-day whether he had heard from their manager, but I was so busy drilling a squad of raw recruits that I didn't get a chance. Guess I'll go to his room now and ask him. I'll have time I think."

As Dick arose there sounded the mournful yet sweet notes of the bugle that was a signal for "lights" out.

"Too late!" exclaimed Paul.

"I'll chance it," ventured Dick. "I can cross to his dormitory by the rear path, and the sentries are hardly posted yet. Besides, I guess they won't report me when they know it's football matters. I'm anxious to know."

"Better stay here—morning will do," counseled Paul.

"No, I'm going, I'll be right back," replied his roommate, and off Dick started before the last notes of the bugle had died away.

Rules regarding being out of the academy after taps were very strict, except at certain times when more liberty was allowed. But this was not one of those occasions, and

Dick knew he would have to be careful. He did not mind indulging in a few pranks occasionally, but now, as he was on the eleven, and captain as well, it behooved him to be careful, so that he would not be barred from athletics.

He swung quietly along the tree-shaded path leading to the dormitory where Hatfield had his rooms. The path was not so well shaded now as in summer, for the trees were almost leafless save for certain oaks, the brown foliage of which rustled in the night wind.

"Sounds like a storm," mused the young millionaire. "I hope it keeps clear long enough for the Haskell game—that is if they'll play us."

As he strolled along he kept a lookout for any sentries, for sometimes new cadets were picked for this duty, and they took delight in reporting their older comrades. But the coast seemed to be clear.

"Guess I'll go see how Grit is, before I go to Hatfield's room," said Dick half aloud, for his pet was now kept in one of the stable barracks. "Poor old fellow, I wish they'd let me keep him with me nights; but they won't."

He swung off in the direction of the building where the cavalry horses were kept, and, as he neared the one where his dog slept he saw a dark figure step out from behind a tree. The figure was that of a cadet with a rifle.

"Hope that's a friend of mine," mused Dick grimly.

A moment later came the command:

"Halt!"

Dick obeyed.

"Who goes there?" was the inquiry as the rifle was swung around.

"Friend."

"Advance friend, and give the countersign."

Dick was startled. Though this was strictly in accordance with the rules, it was something that was seldom enforced. And, to tell the truth, Dick did not have the countersign.

"Well?" came the impatient query. Dick wondered who his challenger could be, for the face was in the shadow.

"I—I'm afraid I haven't the countersign," faltered Dick, who was somewhat annoyed. "Is it actually necessary?"

"Of course it is," was the snapping answer. "Otherwise I shouldn't have asked for it. If you haven't it, you're under arrest."

"I'm Dick Hamilton," said our hero, "and I was on my way to see Hatfield about some football matters. Besides taps have only just sounded."

"Some time ago," was the curt reply. "Besides Hatfield's rooms aren't in the stable."

"I know, but I wanted to see if my dog Grit was safely fastened."

"Oh. Well, I'm sorry," but there was no contrition expressed in the voice, "but I'll have to place you under arrest for trying to run guard, Captain Hamilton," and with that the sentry stepped out from under a tree, revealing himself as Sam Porter.

CHAPTER XVII

UNCLE EZRA ARRIVES

For a moment Dick half thought it was a joke, and he was about to laugh it off. The idea of a member of the football squad—even though temporarily deposed from the team, stopping another team member when on athletic business, even though against the rules, was almost unheard of.

"I guess it's all right—you might remember the countersign for me," said Dick lightly.

"Not much!" snapped Porter.

"Why not?"

"Because I don't choose to. You're under arrest and you will so report to Major Webster.

"Do you mean it?"

"I certainly do."

"But it's—it's so unusual."

"That's just the reason I'm doing it. They make a fellow do guard duty on a frosty night, to catch guard-runners, and then some one kicks when he does it. No, I'm in earnest, and if some of the other fellows who do sentry-go would be the same, they'd stop this. I don't care enough about war tactics to be a sentry, but as long as I am here no one can run the guard on me."

"I wasn't running the guard. I told you where I was going. I want to see if Hatfield had heard from the Haskell team yet."

"And I find you headed toward the stable where your dog is kept, so I can believe you or not as I choose."

Dick started. It was, in a measure telling him that he had not spoken the truth and for a brief moment he felt the hot blood mount to his head. Then he calmed down as he remembered that he was captain of the eleven, and, in a measure responsible to his men for his conduct. Besides, he reflected quickly, Porter might be trying to force him into a quarrel, and that would never do.

"Very well," answered Dick, as quietly as he could, "I'll report to the major. Good night!" He swung on his heel and turned aside.

"Um!" was the only reply that Porter grunted out, as he resumed the patrolling of his post.

"Well?" asked Paul, as his chum entered.

"Not well—bad. I was caught."

"By whom?"

"Porter."

"Porter. Hum! Was he in earnest about it?"

"He seemed so," and Dick recounted the conversation.

"Well, there's something in what he says," agreed Paul. "Sentry-go is no fun, but as long as we're at a military school we have to do it once in a while. Still if enough of us enforced the rules, as I suppose we ought to do, there'd be one of two things happen. They'd either abolish it, or running the guard would stop, and there wouldn't be anything for the sentries to do."

"That's so. Well, I'm the goat to-night. Might as well have a bad job over with. I'm going to report."

"Then you didn't see Hatfield?"

"No, we'll have to wait until morning to hear."

Dick went off in no very happy frame of mind, and he was a little uneasy as to what form of punishment the major would mete out. But he was fortunate in finding that old soldier entertaining a war comrade in his room, and swapping campaign stories. The major was, therefore, in a very amiable mood, and after listening to Dick's frank report said:

"Hum! Well, don't do it again. You may write me out a page of field tactics and consider yourself relieved of arrest. Don't do it again. Good night, Captain Hamilton."

Dick saluted and swung away, highly pleased at the lightness of his task. He heard the major and his comrade-in-arms laughing as he strode away, and the instructor in tactics exclaimed:

"That's not a circumstance to what we used to do, eh, Ned, when we were camped near some city and wanted to go in and have a good time?"

"That's right," agreed his friend.

Dick's little escapade was known all over the academy next morning, and there was almost universal condemnation of Porter's act. But Dick, to the no small astonishment of his chums, declared that the deposed left-end had done just right.

"What are you sticking up for him for?" asked Paul in some indignation. "It'll get so all the other sentries will do the same thing."

"Well, that might not be so bad. Besides, I do think he did right—even though class custom is against it. Then, too, I don't want to get on unfriendly terms with him. I hope to keep in touch with that old miser Duncaster through Porter."

"Oh, yes, about your father's business. How is it coming on?"

"Not very well. I hear that the other side has made a very good offer to Mr. Duncaster, but he has turned them down the same as he did me. There are other matters cropping up, however, that make things complicated in the electric road business, and poor dad is worried to death. I don't know what his next move will be."

"Did you hear whether or not we'll have a game with Haskell?"

"No, but here comes Hatfield now. We'll ask him. He has some mail, perhaps he just heard."

"It's all right!" joyfully called the manager, waving a letter at Dick. "They'll play us next Saturday. Those coaches must have quite a pull."

"Will they put in their first team?" asked Dick anxiously, for there would be little glory in beating the Haskell scrub.

"They'll do that, and also come here to give us a game."

"On our own grounds? Good!" cried Paul. "We'll play our heads off!"

"It's great!" declared Dick. "I only hope we—but there of course we're going to win!" and he changed his sentence with an assumed confidence he hardly felt.

"Will we work any of the new plays on 'em?" asked Paul. "I like the wing shifts and the sequence plays."

"We'll work 'em if we get a chance," said Dick. "It will all depend on what sort of a game they put up. We may have to kick a lot."

"Well, we're up to snuff on that line," declared the manager. "Now I must arrange the details. I hope we get out a big crowd and make some money."

"And I hope the fellows come out to practice this afternoon," spoke Dick. "Come on Paul, we've got the science lecture on now."

The scrub, against whom the Varsity matched forces that afternoon, had been having some secret practice of their own, and they worked a couple of tricks on the rather surprised first team that netted a good gain, and eventually a touchdown.

"That's something you must be on the lookout for," said Mr. Martin, who was a bit chagrined over what had happened. "It isn't enough to play well on your own team, you must watch what the other fellow is doing. Now try again, and put some ginger into your work."

"Yes, you're getting a bit stale I'm afraid," declared Mr. Spencer, and he added some rather sharp words of correction.

The Varsity members were somewhat hurt. They did not know that the words were spoken intentionally, and to force them to do a little better.

The rebuke had the desired effect, and thereafter the unfortunate scrub team was shoved all over the gridiron, not only not getting within striking distance of their opponents' goal line, but having three touchdowns rolled up against them in short order.

"That's something like!" cried Mr. Martin in approval. "Now, Hamilton, try that wing shift," he whispered to Dick. "I think we can fool them."

It was a well executed play, and when the man with the ball got safely away, and through the scrub line Dick slipped and fell, for the ground was soft from a recent rain. Down he went at full length into a puddle, with another player on top of him, and when he arose he was rather a sorry-looking sight, but not injured.

Time was called directly after that, and as the players filed off the field, passing through a little knot of spectators, Dick heard his name called.

"Well, of all the disgraceful sights, you certainly present one!" exclaimed a rasping voice. There was a menancing growl from Grit, whom one of Dick's friends held in leash. Our hero looked toward where the voice had sounded.

"Uncle Ezra!" he faltered, as he saw his grim-visaged relative.

"Yes, I'm here, and I must say of all the brutal exhibitions I ever saw, this is the worst. I never saw a bull fight, but it can't be much worse!"

There was some laughter at this, and Dick looked at his crabbed uncle in some alarm.

"Have you come to see me?" he asked.

"Not exactly. I came because your father is in trouble, and I want to help him."

"Trouble? What kind—the—" began our hero.

"If you'll go somewhere and get washed up, and put some clean clothes on, so you won't look so much like a tramp, I'll talk to you," said Mr. Larabee stiffly. "I've come to take you back home, Nephew Richard."

CHAPTER XVIII

ANOTHER FRUITLESS ATTEMPT

For a moment the young millionaire did not know what to say or think. His father in trouble! Uncle Ezra had come to take him away from Kentfield! And in the height of the football season just before the first big game!

"Is my father ill?" asked Dick.

"No, not ill, only worrying over business. I always said he had too many irons in the fire, and now some have burned him," declared the old man as he walked along beside his nephew out of ear-shot of the crowd. "I've come on to try my hand at helping him."

"But what can you do here?" asked Dick. "And why must I leave Kentfield?"

"To help your father. I should think you'd be glad to. He needs money. It costs money to stay here and play those silly, dangerous games."

"Not very much money, Uncle Ezra."

"Don't tell me! You ought to be in my woolen mill earning four dollars and a quarter a week, instead of wasting cash here. Now I want to have a serious talk with you, Nephew Richard. Your father is in trouble, and it's your duty to leave here and help him."

"I think I can help him by staying here just as well. But did he tell you to take me away from Kentfield—just when I have the football team in good shape? Did he say I was to leave?"

"No, he didn't exactly say so, but I know it would help. Besides, you might get injured playing this game, and then you'd be a cripple for life. You ought to be at work. Now I can make a place for you in the mill. In time you could work up to twelve or fifteen dollars a week, and of course, being my nephew, and the son of my only sister, I'd give you a chance. Better come, Dick. You might be hurt here."

"And I might be hurt in the mill, Uncle Ezra. I have heard of people being caught in the machinery."

"Well, of course it's possible," admitted the crabbed man. "But you must be careful. Besides if you got hurt in the mill it would be in a good cause. Though I warn you I carry accident insurance for all my employees and you can't collect any damages from me."

"Then I think I'll stay and play football, Uncle Ezra."

"Oh, the perversity and foolishness of the rising generation!" groaned Mr. Larabee. "But hurry on and get cleaned up. It is a disgrace for me to be seen walking with you, and I have on my best black suit that I don't want to get spoiled. Besides I must hurry back. I have a lazy hired man that loafs when I'm away."

Dick thought that any hired man who would not take a little chance of resting when his taskmaster was away from home would not show much spirit. But there was Mrs. Larabee to reckon with, and she was almost as much of a "driver" as her husband.

"There, now I am ready to hear all about it," said Dick, when he had led his uncle to one of the reception rooms of the academy, and had removed most of the traces of the recent football conflict. "Are father's affairs in much worse shape?"

"I should say they were!" exclaimed Uncle Ezra. "This man Porter—why Nephew Richard—what is that on your nose?" and the horrified old man sprang from his chair and approached our hero.

"Nose? What's the matter with it?" asked Dick in some alarm.

"There's a great big cut on it! How did it happen?"

"Oh, that's where I tried to stop Hal Foster's shoe with my nose, I expect. That's nothing. It's only a little cut. You should have seen the one I had last year. And when Teddy Naylor broke his collar bone——"

"That's enough! Not another word about the brutalities of football! I've heard enough! It's disgraceful. Let us talk about something else."

"I'm anxious to hear about father's affairs," said Dick.

"I don't know very much," replied his uncle, "but I know that his enemies are pressing him hard to get the control of the trolley line away from him, and it is paying well, too. I never thought it would, but your father insisted that he was right. But he has too many irons in the fire, I'm sure. This time this Mr. Porter is fighting him, and when I saw your father yesterday he said he did not know what to do, because a Mr. Duncaster would not sell his stock."

"Yes, I know that Mr. Duncaster," said Dick, with a grim smile at the recollection of the interview with the man.

"I came here to argue with him," said Mr. Larabee.

"You did?" cried Dick.

"Yes, your father consented. He said you had been unable to do anything with him, and it would do no harm if I tried. I'm a fighter, I am!" and Uncle Ezra squared his jaw aggressively. "I'll make him do as we want him to."

Dick had his doubts about this, but said nothing. He had, moreover, a little feeling against his uncle.

"I want to help dad myself," reflected the young millionaire, "and I believe I can do more with this Mr. Duncaster than Uncle Ezra can. I don't like him 'butting in,' but if dad told him to it must be all right. But I don't believe he'll have much success."

"Now I thought if you could take me to see this person who has the stock," went on Mr. Larabee, "I can induce him to sell it. Once your father has possession of it matters will be all right. Could we go out to his place this afternoon?"

"Oh, yes," agreed Dick. "It is not much of a run to Hardvale."

"I'm glad of it, for then I can start back home to-night. If I take along some sandwiches, which perhaps you can get from the kitchen here for me, I can ride all night in a day coach, and so save a hotel bill. We'll start for Hardvale at once. It is within walking distance, I presume."

"No," answered Dick, and he felt a secret delight in his answer, "the only way to get out there and back in time for you to make an early start for home is to take an auto."

"An auto!" cried Uncle Ezra in horror. "Never! I'll never waste money on one of those affairs, and when I undertook to come here on your father's business I stipulated that I would pay all expenses. He is to give me a commission for doing the work, provided I get the trolley stock, and the less expenses I have the more money I can make."

"But if you don't hire an auto you'll be here so long that you'll have to stay over and pay a hotel bill," said Dick, trying not to smile.

"Couldn't we hire a horse and carriage, or go in a trolley car—trolleys are cheap." Mr. Larabee looked hopeful.

"There is no trolley line to Hardvale," said Dick, "and a horse and carriage would be too slow. It's an auto or a hotel bill, Uncle Ezra."

"Oh dear! What a hard world this is! Well, let us go and get a cheap auto. I'll bargain with the driver."

The chauffeur wanted six dollars to go out to Hardvale and back with his taxicab. At the first mention of the price Dick thought his uncle would have a fit. Then, with a grim tightening of his lips, the old man began to bargain.

"I'll give you two dollars," he said.

"It wouldn't pay for my time, oil and gasolene," declared the man.

"I'll make it three, and not a cent more!" exclaimed Uncle Ezra firmly, with his hand on his pocketbook as if afraid it would be taken away from him.

"You'd better walk!" said the chauffeur. "I haven't any more time to bother with you."

Uncle Ezra begged and pleaded, but the driver was firm.

"Well, I'll tell you what I'll do," said the crabbed old man finally. "I'll pay your price, though I want you to understand that I think it's robbery, but will you throw in some sandwiches for my supper. I'm going to travel all night."

"Oh, yes, I suppose so," finally agreed the chauffeur. "Though it's the first time I've ever given a tip in my own cab. Hop in."

They arrived at Mr. Duncaster's house a little before dusk, and Uncle Ezra rapped on the door. There was a long silence and he knocked again.

"Nobody home I guess," ventured the chauffeur, who was lighting his lamps, preparatory for the trip back.

"Let me try," suggested Dick, and he gave several vigorous blows on the door. Uncle Ezra had rapped lightly, probably so as not to unduly wear out the pair of ancient gloves he was wearing.

This time a window over the front door was opened, and the head of Mr. Duncaster, graced with a nightcap and a tassle, was thrust out.

"What do you want? Go away from here! I've gone to bed!" he shouted. "I'll have you arrested for disturbing the peace! Get away!"

He started to close the window.

"Here! Wait!" cried Mr. Larabee. "I want to talk to you about your trolley stock."

At the mention of stock the window was opened again, and once more the head came out.

"Stock is it? Trolley stock? I suspected it was something like that when I smelled your gasolene wagon coming to my door. Well, that stock isn't for sale, and don't you bother me any more about it. I won't sell to either side. Now you get away. I always go to bed early and it's past my sleeping time now. Get away!"

"But you don't understand!" cried Mr. Larabee in desperation. "We want your stock, and I am authorized to offer you——"

"I won't listen to you! Get away, I'm going to sleep!" The head was drawn in and the window came down with a bang.

"Wait! Hold on! I'll increase the price! I must talk to you!" cried Uncle Ezra, but Mr. Duncaster was firm, and there was no reply to repeated knockings.

"I guess we'd better go," said Dick gently. He had surmised how it would be.

"I'm going to try the back door," said Uncle Ezra craftily. "Maybe I can surprise him." But he had his knocking for his pains, and came back crestfallen.

"Come on," suggested the chauffeur. "I want to get back and do some business where I can make something."

"Humph! You made enough out of us," declared Mr. Larabee as the man cranked up. "Now don't you forget my sandwiches."

They were bowling along through the outskirts of the town when suddenly, around the corner swung another auto. The driver of the one containing Dick and his uncle tried to get out of the way, but it was impossible.

The next instant there was a crash of glass, and Dick found himself sitting on the curbstone, while his uncle with a slight cut over his eye from which the blood was coming, was holding to a street lamppost. Both autos were slightly damaged, but the drivers were not hurt and they proceeded to lay the blame one on the other.

"I'll sue you for this! I'll have damages! I'm an injured man!" cried Uncle Ezra, as he put his handkerchief to his cut eye, while Dick tried to get up, but found that he could not.

"By Jove! I hope my leg isn't broken!" he thought in dismay. "And the Haskell game Saturday! Whew, this is tough luck!"

Once more he made an effort to get up, but fell back in a faint as a sharp pain shot through his ankle. He was conscious of a horrible fear of being disabled, as he felt some one lift his head while a girl's voice exclaimed:

"Why, it's Dick Hamilton! Call a doctor, Mildred." Then Dick lost consciousness.

CHAPTER XIX

A GREAT STRUGGLE

"Don't worry, he'll be all right presently. No, his leg isn't broken—only a slightly sprained ankle. He lost his senses because of the collision shock, as much as from the pain. He's coming around all right."

Dick heard these words as if in a dream. He felt a soft hand on his head—he knew it was that of some girl, but for the life of him he could not tell who it was. He was aware of the smell of pungent drugs, and then he felt some one take hold of his ankle. He uttered a little moan of pain. Then he heard another voice saying, as he opened his eyes:

"Oh, Mildred, he's conscious now."

"Yes, Mabel," answered another girl, and then Dick knew who she was without looking up into the face of the young lady who hastily withdrew her hand from his head.

"Miss Hanford," murmured the young millionaire, as he recognized the girl over whom he and Dutton had so nearly fought a duel in our hero's early cadet days.

"Oh, I'm so glad you know me!" she exclaimed. "Mildred Adams and I were passing along the street just when that dreadful automobile crash came. It's a mercy you weren't all killed."

"Indeed it is!" chimed in Miss Adams. "But Mabel kept her nerves splendidly. She lifted your head, and then she sent me for a doctor."

Dick looked around to observe that he was in the rear room of a drug store, and that a man, evidently a physician, was standing by, regarding him with a professional air.

"Well, young man, how do you find yourself?" asked the doctor.

"Pretty well, as long as nothing is broken."

"No, you're all right that way. You had a lucky escape."

"How is my uncle?" asked the lad anxiously.

"Only a slight cut. The drug clerk is putting some plaster on it. Shall I call him in?"

"Will I be able to play football Saturday?" There was a querulous note in Dick's voice.

"Humph! That's all you lads care about. As soon as you crawl through a knot hole without getting killed you want to rush off to battle. Play Saturday? Well——" The doctor paused.

"I've just *got* to!" cried Dick. "We meet Haskell—it means a lot to my team. I've got to play!"

"Well, I guess we can fix you up if you wear a leather bandage on that ankle. It might be a good deal worse. I'll take another look at it."

"We'll tell that elderly gentleman—your uncle—that you are all right, and ask him to come in here," said Miss Hanford. "Come, Mildred."

They withdrew, and as the physician was tightening the bandages on Dick's ankle Mr. Larabee entered. His appearance was not improved by a large piece of sticking plaster over his right eye, and he looked more aggressive than ever.

"I told you how it would be if we rode in one of them automobiles!" he exclaimed. "It's all your fault, Nephew Richard, and you'll have to pay the doctor bills. I shan't, and what's more I shan't pay that driver either. He ought to be more careful."

"Please don't get excited," begged the doctor, with a regard for Dick's nerves.

"I'm not excited!" cried Uncle Ezra, "but I know my rights and I want 'em, too! I'm not excited, but I'll have the law on that murdering villain of an automobile man! I'll sue 'em both. I'll collect damages. We'll see if there's any justice in this land!" and he smote his clenched right fist into the open palm of his left hand. "I'll have my rights. I'm not excited, but I'll have justice."

"All right, Uncle Ezra," spoke Dick calmly. "Is the chauffeur hurt?"

"I don't care whether he is or not. I'll have the law——"

"I'm all right—only some bruises. It was that other fellow's fault, he was on the wrong side of the street. Are you all right, Mr. Hamilton?" asked the chauffeur, at that moment entering the room. He knew Dick, having driven him about many times.

"Glad you're not injured," spoke the lad. "Is your machine in shape to run? I want to get back to the academy. The fellows may hear about this and think I'm worse hurt than I am. Can you take me back?"

"Sure. Only my front lights, and some of the glass windows were smashed. I'll run you back."

"Nephew Richard, do you mean to say you're going to ride back in that miserable man's machine?" demanded Mr. Larabee.

"Why certainly," replied the young millionaire calmly, as he arose from the couch on which he had been lying. The doctor assisted him. "Why shouldn't I go back that way. I don't want to use my ankle more than I have to before the game."

"Well, all I've got to say is that you're more foolhardy than I thought you were, and I wash my hands of the whole affair," said Uncle Ezra bitterly. "I'm going back home and report to your father. I'm sorry I couldn't do anything with Mr. Duncaster, but he is an obstinate man. And what's more, I won't pay hire for that automobile, either."

"Yes, you will!" cried the driver.

"That will be all right," spoke Dick quickly, making the driver a concealed motion, which the man understood.

"I'm going back to Dankville," went on the crabbed old man, "and I hope I never have to leave it again. My nerves are all shattered by what I've gone through, and if I'm a physical wreck as I expect to be after this accident I'll sue you for heavy damages," he threatened, to the auto driver.

"Go ahead," was the calm reply. Then, after he had bidden Dick a rather cool good-bye, Uncle Ezra departed. He did not ask for the sandwiches for his lunch, and Dick wondered at it.

"A strange character—rather strong-willed I should say," observed the physician, when Uncle Ezra had gone.

"Yes," agreed Dick simply. He rather thought his uncle might have remained to see that he got to his room safely. But since the attempted kidnapping affair there had been more coldness than ever between Dick and his aged relative.

"Are you feeling strong enough to be moved?" asked the doctor.

"Oh, yes, and I'm much obliged to you."

"You also have the young ladies to thank," spoke the medical man with a smile.

"Oh, of course," assented our hero. He managed by the help of the chauffeur to limp out to the waiting taxicab. Miss Hanford and Miss Adams were in the drug store.

"I can't thank you enough for your first-aid-to-the-injured services," said Dick with a smile, as he shook hands with the young ladies. "It was very good of you."

"Oh, you're not done with us yet," said Miss Hanford gaily. "I've telephoned for my cousin Harold, and he's going to go to the academy with you. He'll be here in a few minutes. Here he is now," she added, as a tall, good-looking lad entered the store. Mabel introduced him to Dick, and though our hero insisted that he could get along well enough with the help of the chauffeur, Harold Johnson insisted on accompanying him in the cab.

"Let us know how you are?" called Mabel after them, as they started off, the crowd that had gathered dispersing, now that the excitement was over.

"Well old man, you certainly had a time of it!" exclaimed Paul Drew, when young Johnson had safely delivered his charge and departed. "What are you trying to do, anyhow?"

"I don't know. It all came so suddenly there was no time to do anything. I'm sorry about Mr. Duncaster though. I wish Uncle Ezra had not butted in, for now it will make it all the harder for me when I try again to get that stock."

"Are you going to try again?"

"Surely. Dad needs it. But I'm not going to worry about that now. We've got to devote all our attention to the Haskell game."

"Do you think you can play?"

"I'm going to!" declared Dick fiercely.

He received visits from every member of the eleven and most of the substitutes before taps that night, and they were all relieved when they found that the young captain's injuries were not as severe as had at first been reported.

Dick was not able to practice the next day, but the following one he was on the gridiron, and he was delighted to find that, aside from a little stiffness, his ankle did not trouble him.

"Fellows, this is your last chance," declared Coach Martin, the day previous to the great Haskell game. "Make good now and——"

"To-morrow," put in Mr. Spencer with a smile. "And don't forget that you're going to win!"

In spite of a slight pain in his ankle, Dick never ran the team to better advantage than he did in practice that day.

"Oh, for to-morrow!" he exclaimed to Paul in their room that night.

What crowds there were! They overflowed the grandstands and surged upon the space around the Kentfield gridiron. They stood several deep along the ropes stretched to keep them back, and still they poured through the entrance gates to the delight of the cadets.

"We'll make some money all right off this game!" exulted Manager Hatfield. "And we need it, even if we have a millionaire on the team."

"No, we can't expect Dick to do it all," said Paul.

"He's mighty good to hire the coaches," commented George Hall. "Oh, say, if we can only win! Has the Haskell bunch arrived yet?"

"No, but they'll soon be here. Come on, our fellows are going to get in practice."

Out on the field trotted the Kentfield eleven, with the score of substitutes, wrapped, Indian-like in blankets, squatting on the side lines, until such time as they would be needed to form some opposition for the Varsity.

This soon came, for the coaches, after putting the boys through some recently evolved formations, called on the scrub. Then the practice was harder.

A roar burst from a thousand throats as the Haskell team trotted out, for they had brought many supporters with them. Then came cheer after cheer—cheers for Kentfield and for their opponents.

"They're a husky lot all right," observed Dutton grimly, as the Kentfield cadets ceased their practice to "size-up" their foes.

"And beefy," added John Stiver.

"Oh, say, don't get heart-disease so soon," advised Dick with a laugh. "Wait until you see us walk through 'em."

The preliminaries were soon arranged, and luck was with Dick for he won the toss and selected the east goal, with what wind there was in his favor. This gave the ball to Haskell to be kicked off, and a few minutes later, the twenty-two sturdy youths took the field. Dick placed his men with care, and gave an anxious look all about him, as the Haskell centre "teed" the new yellow ball on a little mound of earth on the middle line.

Shrilly blew the whistle, and a moment later there was a dull "thump!" as the toe of the big centre rush found the pigskin, and sent it well into Kentfield's territory. Ray Dutton caught it, and, tucking the spheroid under his arm he sprinted down over the chalkmarks, gathering speed at every stride.

"Cover him, fellows! Cover him!" yelled Dick, and the right half-back's supporters gathered in front of him as well as they could. But the opposition streamed through. Dutton ran on until in front of him loomed Peters, the gigantic right guard of Haskell, and then the plucky cadet ran no more, for he was heavily thrown. But the ball had been carried back to Kentfield's forty-yard mark.

"Line up, boys!" yelled Dick. "Go through 'em now."

He stooped down behind Jim Watkins, and began calling the signal for Stiver to circle Haskell's right wing. Back came the ball, and Stiver got it on the jump, but so fast did the opponents of Kentfield stream around to meet him that he did not gain more than three yards.

"They're strong!" murmured Dick with a bit of despondency in his voice, for he had seen how in vain his men hurled themselves against the stone-wall-like line of Haskell.

"So much the more credit if we beat them!" whispered Paul.

The captain was half decided on a try around the other end, but a movement in the line told him this was almost suspected so he called for a fake kick with Dutton to take the ball.

The spheroid came back true, and John tucked it against his chest as, with head well down, he hurled himself forward. But the hole was not there, and once more the enemies of Kentfield got through so that only two yards were made.

"We've got to punt," thought Dick, as he gave the signal.

Straight and true the ball sailed from the toe of Hal Foster's shoe—far into the territory of Haskell, so far indeed that their full-back had to retreat to gather it in. Back he sprinted, protected by his eager mates.

"Get to him, boys! Get to him!" pleaded Dick, and into the knot of players rushed Beeby, Drew and Hall. Hall was shoved aside and Paul Drew was put out of business, but Beeby dodged through, and, a moment later, his powerful arms circled his man—the man with the ball. Down they went in a heap.

A few seconds later the offensive tactics of Haskell were in operation, and powerful they were. First came a smashing attack between left guard and centre that netted five yards. Once more the line was bucked, and through left guard and tackle came hurtling the man with the ball. Another gain was netted around right end, and then came a line play on the other side. Kentfield was being pushed back, and thus far her opponents had found no necessity for kicking.

"Hold 'em! Hold 'em!" pleaded Dick. "Brace!"

His men tried, and with such power on the next play that only one yard was made.

"That's it!" cried the captain gleefully.

On the side lines the coaches watched the struggle.

"I'm afraid they're too much for 'em," murmured Mr. Martin regretfully.

"Yes, perhaps, but the game is young yet, and it's full of chances. Besides, did you note the brace they took?"

"Yes—it's great—we'll have a fine team before the season is over."

Smash and bang went the attack on Dick's line. He did all that mortal captain could do to infuse some of his own strength and courage into his men, but it seemed that it was not to be. Down the field the ball was rushed until it was within thirty yards of the Kentfield goal.

"Touchdown! Touchdown!" demanded the crowd in sympathy with Haskell.

"Hold boys, hold!" yelled the Kentfield adherents and they sang cheering songs and gave their school war-cries.

"Don't let 'em through!" almost tearfully pleaded Dick, though it seemed that a score was inevitable. "Brace! Brace!"

Once more a hammer-like attack, and the ball was on Kentfield's twenty-two yard line. Then it looked as if at the next play either a try for goal would be made, or that some lucky player on Haskell would smash through and dodge his way to a touchdown.

But something happened. Through some miscalculation when Haskell's quarter got ready to pass the ball on the next play he found his man missing, through inattention to the signal. Thereupon the quarter ran with it himself, without having covered the necessary five yards to one side. This carried with it a penalty which sent the ball back to Kentfield's thirty-seven yard line, and Dick breathed easier. The almost inevitable was postponed for a little while.

A forward pass was next attempted by Haskell, but the memory of the recent fizzle must have been on the minds of her players, for the ball was juggled. Perkins, the left guard fell on it, and then, after a hurried line-up, Matthews, the full-back, tried for a goal from the thirty-five yard line.

The ball rose well, for he was amply protected, and a yell of delight came from a thousand throats as Haskell's supporters thought they saw their side scoring. But Matthews did not have good aim, and the ball struck the posts and bounded back where Dick got it.

"Our ball!" cried Dick in delight, as the pigskin was brought out to the Kentfield twenty-five yard line.

"Are you going to kick?" whispered Paul.

"No, we'll buck the line again. I think they're tired."

The captain's judgment was vindicated, for on a wing shift Ray Dutton went through for ten yards, and at this unexpected breaking up of the powerful line of Haskell there were roars of delight from the home crowd.

Again Dick sent a man smashing through with the ball, and the opponents were tumbled to one side, for the Kentfield guards and tackle were fierce now with the desire for revenge, and they tore great gaps in the ranks of the men before them.

A fake kick gained another substantial distance, and then misfortune came, for there was holding by some of Dick's men, and they lost the ball on a penalty. But so far had they advanced it into the territory of their enemies that the Haskell captain ordered a kick. Dick saw their game now.

"They think to tire us, for, they think I'll begin smashing their line again. Then, at the close of the half they'll knock us all apart," he reasoned as he helped form interference for Foster, who had caught the ball.

"Instead of that we'll kick!" instantly decided Dick. "That will keep the ball in their territory, but if they send it back I'll chance some more smashes."

He called to the full-back to boot the leather forward, and back it came with unerring aim. It was somewhat of a surprise to Haskell, and they were a bit demoralized, for they had not expected such fierce playing, nor such good generalship. Then followed another punt from the Haskell full-back, and Stiver caught the ball.

"Rush it back!" ordered Dick, his voice scarcely heard above the tumult.

Stiver was shortly downed, but Kentfield had the ball, and once more began to smash at the line with all the fierceness of which she was capable. Haskell was plainly taken by surprise, but they held their opponents to advantage and in two downs only ten yards were gained. A kick was inevitable, and it came.

This time, after rushing the ball back until downed Haskell tried some new tactics. They worked a neat forward pass, and an adaptation of the wing shift so that in a few minutes Kentfield's goal was again menaced.

"Now's the time to hold again!" cried Dick, and hold they did, until Stiver was injured and had to leave the game. Ford Endton was called in, and then the smashing went on once more.

Slowly Kentfield was being pushed back, and about all Dick could hope for was the whistle that would announce the end of the half, for that would save being scored on.

Once more fate came to his aid. There was off-side play on the part of Haskell, and one of her men was detected "slugging". As a result Kentfield got the ball, and her opponent was penalized ten yards. Dick promptly ordered a kick, and the pigskin was sent whizzing down the field into Haskell territory.

Haskell at once kicked back, but gained little, and then Dick called for some more line plays. It was a bad move, as the ball could not be advanced and Dick had to kick again. Then back at the wearied Kentfield players came burrowing and boring their enemies, until our friends were shoved back up the field.

Nearer and nearer to their own goal they were pushed, until the ball was within five yards of it. Dick begged and pleaded, but it is likely that not all the urging in the world could have prevented a touchdown, only that the whistle blew, ending the half, and the tired players rushed from the field.

"Well, we didn't score," remarked Dick somewhat gloomily to the coaches who hurried out to him.

"Score? Nobody expected you would against that team!" cried Mr. Martin. "But look what you did. You equaled them all around, and they couldn't score on you."

"They feel worse than you do!" exclaimed Mr. Spencer. "You boys did nobly. I fancy Blue Hill is trembling at this moment."

"I hope so," said Dick. "But I want to score next half."

The rest, and the words of praise showered on them from all sides at the plucky game they had put up, did much to put heart into our heroes. They went back into the contest with an eagerness that was a delight to the coaches and their captain.

An exchange of kicks followed the second half initial send-off, and when Dick's team got the ball they once more tried their bucking. The first try, however showed that Haskell's line had been much strengthened, and this was because several new players had gone in, whereas, with the exception of two, the Kentfield team was the same.

"They're afraid of us!" Dick whispered in delight to Paul. "They held out some of their best players—now they have them in. We're up against the strongest team they have," and this was so.

Wishing to save his men as much as possible, Dick called for some wing-shift and fake-kick plays that proved to be good ground-gainers. But there was a fumble in one, and Haskell got the ball.

Her smashing attack proved the virtue of the new players, and in less than ten minutes of play in the second half the ball had been shoved over for a touchdown, and the goal was kicked.

"Oh, but that's tough!" sighed Innis.

"It might be worse!" said Dick, as cheerfully as he could. "We're holding them well, considering the new men they have, but we're going to score now."

He and his men made a good try for it. They got the ball on a fumble after some play following the touchdown, and began to rush it back. For a moment their attack was so irresistible that Haskell crumpled to pieces. Then, maddened and ashamed at

112 | P a g e

having a smaller-sized team treat them thus, they braced, and the advance of Kentfield was stopped.

Again Haskell came smashing at Dick's line. He knew what it meant. They were determined to have another touchdown and the plucky captain was just as determined not to let them get it. But it seemed as if it must come.

Smash, bang! Smash, bang! came the heart-breaking attack. Haskell was so sure of herself now that she did not kick. But she was a little too sure, for she held in the line again, and the ball came to our friends. It was promptly punted out of danger, but instead of returning the punt Haskell once more came back to the banging tactics.

"Another touchdown!" was the demand.

"Never! Never!" thought Dick in desperation.

The ball was within ten yards of his line. He knew there could be but a few minutes more of play.

"Hold 'em fellows, hold!" he implored. "If we can keep 'em down to one touchdown it's as good as a victory for us!"

Hold the Kentfield cadets did, though slowly but surely they were being shoved back. They even dug their hands into the dirt until their nails bled, but it seemed useless.

"Now boys for a touchdown!" called the Haskell captain with a laugh. "We're going to get it, too!" he added, looking Dick straight in the face.

The signal came. Into the line came smashing the man with the ball—straight through a hole that had been torn with savage energy between Drew and Watkins. Straight at Dick the man came, Haskell's big guard. Dick tackled him like a tiger, and felt himself being bowled over. A sharp pain shot through his injured ankle, and he knew the bandage had slipped. But he also knew something else, for the ball had bounced from the grasp of the guard and lay within reach of our hero.

He pulled himself from underneath the husky guard, though the pain in his foot was excruciating, and like a flash was up. Then, before any one knew what he was doing, he had booted the ball well down the field, though the kick cost him unbearable pain. But he had saved another touchdown against his team, for at that moment the final whistle blew, and the great game was over.

CHAPTER XX

JOINING THE LEAGUE

They had to carry Dick off the field, but there was a happy smile on his face in spite of the terrible pain of his injured ankle.

"Only one touchdown and a goal against us, and the best team Haskell could put in the field, fellows!" exulted the plucky captain. "It's almost as good as a victory."

"There could be no more honorable defeat," murmured Coach Martin.

"I should say not!" exclaimed his colleague. "Our work hasn't gone for nothing."

"Let me congratulate you, Captain Hamilton!" cried the captain of Haskell, as he strode up to shake Dick's hand. "We sure thought we would wipe up the earth with you, but—well, we were astonished, to put it mildly."

"We'll beat you next time," said Dick simply.

"I shouldn't be surprised but what you did," he agreed. "You certainly have improved wonderfully. Where'd you get those coaches?" for the two had walked on in advance.

"Oh, they were a sort of an experiment," answered the young millionaire, "but it worked out all right. Kentfield needed some improvement and——"

"She's more than got it!" cried the other captain. "Boys, three cheers for the pluckiest team we ever went up against!" he called, and how the cries rang out; bringing joy and a mist of tears to the eyes of our injured hero.

"Three cheers for Haskell!" called Dick in return, and the compliment was given.

"We'd have scored again but for that plucky tackle of yours, and your kick," said the guard whom Dick had thrown in the nick of time. "Hurt yourself much?"

"No, it's only where I twisted my ankle before. I'll be all right in a few days, and ready for more games."

The crowd was thronging from the field, as Dick was carried into the dressing room. There some hot applications, and skillful bandaging, put his ankle in such shape that he could manage to get around on a cane that some one provided.

"It was great! Great, old man!" cried Paul, circling in delight about his chum. "I never thought we could do it. Did you really think we would win? I hope you're not disappointed."

"Only a little," admitted Dick. "I hoped we might win up to the time I saw their team come out on the field. Then I knew they were too much for us. But we held them down!"

"Indeed we did."

"And the next thing to do is to get into the Military League, and wipe out the unnecessary insult that Blue Hill handed to us, by giving them the worst drubbing they ever had."

"Sure," assented Paul.

There was quite a crowd of hero-worshippers outside the dressing rooms, waiting to get a sight of Dick and his men, and cheer them. Among the throng our hero espied a pretty face he knew, and straightway he made for it as well as he was able.

"Congratulations!" called Miss Hanford. "Oh, it was a glorious game! but I'm so sorry you were hurt."

"It's nothing," murmured Dick gamely, though as he spoke a spasm of pain shot through him.

There were not a few on the hospital list as a result of the Haskell-Kentfield game and in view of that, and the great work that had been done, practice was omitted for a few days. When it was resumed it was light, for there were several of the best players, besides the captain, to be considered, and good men were scarce.

On all sides among the various groups of cadets there was heard nothing but praise for Dick's team. Only one little crowd had anything unpleasant to say, and this was the faction headed by Porter.

"If Porter had played there wouldn't have been so many gains around left end," said one of the rich lad's cronies.

"That's right," added Weston. "Porter was our mainstay before he got put off by Hamilton's influence."

"Who says by Dick's influence?" demanded Paul Drew hotly.

"I do!"

"Then you don't know what you're talking about, and I advise you not to repeat it," spoke Dick's chum grimly, and Weston slunk away.

But what little feeling there was died away in the memory of the glorious game that had been played, and even some of the instructors were enough interested in athletics to congratulate Dick and his chums.

"What's the next move?" asked Paul of his roommate, as they sat in the precincts of the Sacred Pig one night, talking over matters of the gridiron.

"Well, we ought to join the Military League, I think. We are practically out of it through the refusal of Blue Hill to accept our challenge, and I presume we'll have to join over again," was the opinion of Dutton.

"That's right!" cried Dick.

"Will they let us in?" asked George Hall.

"They'll have to," was what Manager Hatfield said. "I am going to have a consultation with the coaches to-morrow, and we'll decide on what to do. If we are admitted, as I have no doubt we will be, we'll challenge Blue Hill Academy again."

A correspondence was at once begun with the necessary officers of the league, and it was carried on to such advantage that inside of a week Kentfield was formally notified of her election to the organization. This was composed of several military academies, as I have said, and the winning of the football championship carried with it the possession of a gold loving cup.

Hard practice was the rule for the next few days, and then came a game with Mooretown which Kentfield won. The next week she played a small team, not in the league, and the week following came a contest with Richmore, one of the tail-enders of the league. This resulted in a big victory for Kentfield, and further advanced her prestige.

"Have you challenged Blue Hill yet?" asked Dick of the manager one day.

"I'm going to this week. I think we've won our spurs now. How is your ankle, if we do play?"

"Fine as a fiddle. I've taken the bandage off. Oh, we'll play for our lives when we meet those fellows!"

Blue Hill could now have no reason for refusing to meet Kentfield, and though they offered no apology for their former sarcastic letter, they accepted the challenge.

Dick was with Manager Hatfield when the answering missive was received.

"That's the stuff!" cried the young millionaire. "Now we'll practice harder than ever."

Toots, the janitor, approached our hero, whistling "In the Prison Cell I Sit." He saluted and seemed to want to say something.

"What is it?" asked Dick.

"I've just got word, Mr. Hamilton, that your dog Grit has been arrested—or, that is, taken to the pound for going about without his license tag on, which is against the law," said the janitor.

"Grit taken to the pound! Who did it?" cried Dick.

"Some fellow by the name of Duncaster," was the unexpected reply. "He had a policeman take the dog in, and you have to pay ten dollars to get him out. Half of it goes to that Duncaster man for causing the dog to be taken in."

"Duncaster!" murmured Dick. "He's fighting us all along the line! I'm going to town!" he called to a group of his chums who had gathered about him.

"I'll go with you," and Paul hastened after his friend.

CHAPTER XXI

READY FOR BLUE HILL

Dick was half wrathful over the action of Mr. Duncaster, and half because of the action of some cadet who must have enticed Grit to town, for a few students, admiring the bulldog had, in times past, often led him off with them. Nor was Grit unwilling to go, for he loved action, and by reason of his lessons and his football practice his master had little time to take him out.

"What are you going to do?" asked Paul, as his chum swung around toward the stable.

"I'm going to find out who took my dog to town, and then I'm going after him," was the answer. "He had nerve, who ever he was."

"Do you think Duncaster did it? Because he knew it was your animal?"

"He may have done so, but I doubt it. He's just naturally mean and cranky, and when he found Grit wandering about the street he probably notified a dog-catcher. I didn't think they were so strict when cool weather set in. Poor Grit! In a pound with a lot of curs! His feelings will be hurt."

In answer to Dick's inquiries one of the stable men stated that Cadet Porter had come and gotten Grit, leading him off by a leash attached to his collar.

"Did he say I said for him to take Grit?" asked the young millionaire.

"No, sir, I can't say as how he did. But he's been real friendly with the dog, Mr. Porter has, and Grit knows him. Mr. Porter and Mr. Weston went off together with him. I hope you don't blame me, Mr. Hamilton," and the man seemed a bit alarmed.

"No, it wasn't your fault. But, after this, please don't let any one take Grit without my permission. First thing I know he'll be stolen, and then Uncle Ezra will be as happy as a lark."

On the way to town Dick and Paul met Porter and Weston returning. The faces of both were flushed, and they were smoking cigarettes. Porter seemed ill at ease as he encountered Dick, and the latter resolving to settle the matter once and for all said:

"What right had you to take my dog, Porter?"

"I'm mighty sorry, Ham," was the contrite answer, and for a change Porter was not blustering and overbearing as he usually was. "You see I took him in, as I've done once before, and you didn't mind, but——"

"Yes, but this time I *do* mind!" exclaimed Dick sharply. "He got away from you, didn't he?"

"Yes, I tied him to the leg of the billiard table, while I shot a match with Weston. Beat him, too, and I must have felt so jolly over it that I forgot about Grit. When I went to look for him he was gone—he'd slipped out of his collar. I guess he was lonesome for you. He got home all right, I hope."

"No, he didn't!" replied Dick in no gracious tones.

"He didn't?" Porter was manifestly surprised.

"He's in the pound, and I have to pay ten dollars to get him out."

"Whew! That's tough luck! I'm mighty sorry about it. If I wasn't so counfoundedly short of funds now I'd give you the money for the fine right away. As it is I'll owe it to you."

"No, you won't!" cried our hero sharply. "I'll pay it myself, but don't take Grit away again—please." He added the last as he happened to remember that he was captain of the football team, and that Weston, Porter's crony, was a member of the eleven, and that Porter might also play later. It would not do to be on bad terms with them, for the sake of the team.

"Oh, well, you needn't be stiff about it," murmured Porter. "I didn't mean any harm. How did I know the dog would get away."

"You didn't, I presume," agreed Dick, a little mollified. "But don't do it again. Come on, Paul."

"You cad!" muttered Porter, as Dick swung around. "I'm beginning to hate you! I'll get even, some day too. You put me off the team!"

"Oh, I wouldn't feel that way," suggested Weston, who was not a half-bad chap. "You may get a chance yet."

"Not after this blamed dog incident. Why didn't you have an eye on the brute?"

"Why should I? It was your affair."

"Oh, well, if that's the way you feel about it, don't come with me again!" snapped Porter, who was in ill humor.

The pound of the town was in a stable back of one of the police stations, and there Dick found Grit chained up with several other dogs of much lower degree.

"Hello, old boy!" greeted the lad, and Grit nearly broke the chain to leap upon his master.

"Be careful," warned the poundkeeper. "He's got an ugly temper."

"Not when he's treated right," was the answer. "I'll take him along. Here's his collar," for Porter had handed it over before parting from Dick. "I'll take him home. To whom do I pay the ten dollars?"

"To me. Half goes to the town and the other half to the man who caused the dog to be taken in. Rumcaster is his name, or something like that. He's been here several times since the dog was brought in, asking if the fine was paid. He wants his share, Mr. Rumcaster does."

"Duncaster is my name! Duncaster!" exclaimed a rasping voice, and the man who had been so unpleasant to Dick made his appearance. "And so the dog's owner is here, is he? I guess this will be a lesson to him. Where's my five dollars?"

"Here!" exclaimed Dick suddenly stepping forward.

"Ah, ha! So it's that Hamilton soldier fellow!" exploded Enos Duncaster, as he saw our hero. "It was your dog; eh? You should know better than to let unmuzzled and unlicensed dogs run loose in the streets. But it's what might be expected of a young man who goes to school to learn a murdering trade. Bah! I'm glad it *was* your dog!"

"The dog is licensed, and was running loose because the cadet who took him without my permission did not take care of him," answered Dick quietly.

"Hum! I can't help that young man! The law is the law and I'm entitled to my five dollars. It will keep me in groceries for a week. I don't eat much!" and the old man chuckled grimly as he pocketed the bill, and tottered off on his cane.

"Come on Grit, old boy!" called Dick, as he paid over the other five dollars, and led the now rejoicing animal away.

The young millionaire tried not to feel any resentment against Porter, but it was hard work. Not so much on account of the ten dollars, as because of what might have happened to Grit. On his part Porter was cooler than ever toward Dick, but it did not so much matter as our hero had learned all he could about the financial operations of the rich lad's father,—and since he knew who held the large number of shares of electric stock.

"Not that it's doing dad much good to know," mused the young millionaire, "for Duncaster will be more against me than ever now, I'm afraid. He won't even listen to me."

Fortunately the necessity for hard work on the gridiron gave Dick so much to think about that he did not have much time to worry over this matter, though he made up his mind to aid his father whenever opportunity presented.

Hard practice was called for, in preparation for the Blue Hill game, and the young captain and the coaches were glad to see the snappy playing, and the aggressive spirit manifested.

"I think we can defeat them, after what we did to Haskell," said Dick.

"I do also," agreed Mr. Martin, and Mr. Spencer was no less positive.

It was three days before the game, and the boys were "on edge" and fit to make the battle of their lives. That night Dick was paying a visit in the rooms of Innis Beeby, when George Hall came in.

"What's the matter up in your bungalow?" asked Jim Watkins, coming in during a deep discussion of a new wing shift play.

"Nothing—why?" asked Dick quickly.

"I thought you might be sick. I just saw Dr. Fenwick going in there," was the answer. "But you seem healthy enough."

"Dr. Fenwick—going to our room!" cried Dick, starting up. "It must be Paul. He wasn't feeling well this evening, and wouldn't come out with me. I'll go see!" and he hastened away.

CHAPTER XXII

THE BLUE HILL GAME

The thoughts of the young captain were rather alarming as he made his way to the apartment he shared with his chum. He had paid little attention to the complaint Paul made of not feeling well, thinking it was only a temporary indisposition. That had been several hours before, for time had passed quickly in the room of Innis, with the spirited talk of football.

"And he had to send for a doctor when I wasn't there with him!" exclaimed Dick to himself regretfully. "That was tough. But I kept thinking he'd join us every minute or I'd gone back. I hope it isn't anything serious."

Then he recalled several stories he had read of football players being secretly "doped" before big games in order that they would go "stale" and not be in form.

"That may have happened to Paul!" half-gasped the young captain. "Some of those Blue Hill fellows, fearing we will beat them, may have sent him some dope. If they have——"

Then Dick laughed at his preposterous fears, and by this time he was at his room. Behind the closed door he heard the murmur of voices. One he recognized as that of his chum, and the other was Dr. Fenwick's.

"Well, he's alive at any rate," thought the young millionaire. "He can't be so bad."

Nevertheless it was rather an alarmed countenance of Dick Hamilton that gazed in on his chum a moment later. Paul was in bed, and in the room was one of the academy orderlies, while the physician was bending over a table, mixing some medicine in a glass.

"Paul!" cried Dick impulsively. "What's the matter? Jim Watkins just told me Dr. Fenwick was here. How did it happen? What is the matter? I'm so sorry I left you alone, but I thought every minute that you'd be over. I'm all cut up about it."

"It's all right, Dick, old man," replied Paul, but in fainter tones than he was in the habit of using. "I'm just a little under the weather I guess. I'll be on the active list again soon."

"I hope so," murmured the captain, with the memory of the impending Blue Hill game. Paul was one of his best players—one who could always be depended on in an emergency—one who always had some "go" left in him, when it seemed that mortal flesh and bone could do no more. He could tear through the line, and break up interference better than any guard Dick had ever seen, and for nailing the man with the ball Paul was a star. No wonder the young captain did not want to lose him.

"Is it anything serious, Doctor?" asked Dick.

"I hope not," replied Dr. Fenwick. "I don't like some of his symptoms, but they may pass away."

"How did it happen—how did it come on?" inquired the young millionaire.

"Oh, I hadn't felt well all day," replied the plucky left guard, "but I didn't think anything of it. Then a little while ago I suddenly felt dizzy, and before I knew what was happening I keeled over—fell on the floor. Brooks, in the next room, heard me, and came rushing in. He got the doctor—that's all I know."

"And I wasn't here?" exclaimed Dick reproachfully.

"I fancy it is only due to an upset condition of the stomach," put in the physician. "He has an attack of vertigo, which is not uncommon. There, Mr. Drew, I'll leave this medicine, and look in on you in the morning. If you need me in the night don't hesitate to send for me."

"I'll look after him," promised Dick. The physician and orderly were about to leave when several of the cadets who had been in Beeby's room, and who wondered at Dick's sudden desertion, came trooping in, to ask all sorts of questions concerning Paul.

"Now, young gentlemen, this won't do!" insisted the doctor cheerfully but firmly. "Mr. Drew must be kept quiet. He is in no danger, and you'll have to leave."

They did, after nodding pleasantly to the sick lad, and then Dick began a vigil of the night.

"Jove! I hope Drew doesn't go back on us in the Blue Hill game," remarked Dutton.

"It would sort of break us up, even though Berkfeld fills in pretty well at guard," spoke George Hall.

As for the worriment of the young captain, only he himself realized the depth of it.

Paul was restless all night, and had a slight fever. Dick was a faithful nurse, administering the medicine regularly. Once his patient was delirious, and murmured something about matters at home. Again he fancied himself on the gridiron, and called out:

"Touchdown! Touchdown! We've got to make a touchdown! That's it. Go through the line now!"

"Poor Paul," murmured Dick. "I'm afraid it will be quite a while before you play again."

Twice, when the lad's condition seemed worse, Dick was on the point of sending for Dr. Fenwick, but he refrained and the spell passed over.

Morning came, pale and wan, shining in the room where the electric lights burned with a sickly glow. Dick turned them out and softly laid his hands on Paul's cheek.

"He seems cooler," he whispered. "I believe the fever has gone down. I hope it has. He's sleeping soundly. I—I believe I'll lie down for a moment."

Dick himself felt weak, for he had been up nearly all night, and the day before he had practiced strenuously. He stretched out on the lounge, and before he knew it he was sleeping soundly. He awakened as a voice called faintly:

"Is there any water handy, Dick?"

"Paul! How are you?" he cried, springing up. "Oh, I must have dozed off! That was careless of me. Are you all right? I'm a swell nurse, I am."

"Oh, don't worry. I'm much better, and I'm hungry and thirsty."

"That's a good sign. I'll get some fresh water."

Paul drank eagerly, and Dick, taking his temperature with the thermometer the physician had left, was glad to note that the little silver column was at ninety-eight and three-fifths, or normal.

"Your fever's gone!" he announced, with a thrill in his tired voice.

Dr. Fenwick came in a little later, and seconded the opinion Dick had formed. Paul was weak, but the danger had passed, he announced.

"It must have been something he ate," was what the doctor said, and Dick thought no more about "dope."

"Will I be able to play Saturday?" asked Paul eagerly.

"Humph! Yes, I think so, if you get back your strength. You lost considerable in a short time. But take it easy at first."

They missed Paul at practice that day, and as Dick was somewhat worn with his sleepless night, the coaches did not insist on very strenuous work. What was done, however, showed that the Kentfield eleven was holding its own.

Paul was out the next day, and did light work. He was a bit "off his feed" as he expressed it, but he was sure he would be all right when it came to the big game.

Little was talked of in the academy but the coming contest, which was to take place on the Kentfield gridiron. Some of the sporting crowd had what they called "big money" up on the game, but few of the football contingent indulged in this practice.

"I got odds of two to one from some of the Blue Hill crowd," boasted Porter, who had a liking for betting. "I could have gotten bigger odds before the Haskell fight, but the Blue Hill fellows are a bit shy now. I should think you'd back your own team, Hamilton," he said, with a half sneer at Dick.

"It isn't in my line," was the answer, "though I've no objections to you fellows backing us for all you're worth. We'll come in winners, I'm sure."

"I wish I could play," spoke Porter more earnestly than he was in the habit of doing. "Is there any chance for me, Hamilton?" He had effectually put his pride in his pocket to thus appeal to the lad who for no cause he disliked.

"I wish there was," answered the captain. "Of course you will have the same chance as the other subs, and if the fight is as rough as I expect it will be, we may be playing all of you before it's over."

"Then I can't go in at the opening?"

"I don't see how you can very well. Of course I haven't it all to say. Why don't you go see the coaches?"

"What good would that do. They're in your pay, and——"

"That will do!" cried Dick sharply, and Porter knew enough to stop that sort of talk. He turned away, a bitter look on his face and a bitter feeling in his heart.

"I'll get even with you yet," he muttered. "I'll fix you and your football team, Dick Hamilton!"

Dick was like some anxious mother the night before the game. He went to the rooms of each of his players and saw that they were in. Inquiries as to how they felt met with the reply that they were all "fit."

Paul Drew seemed himself again, and assured Dick that he was ready to do battle with their common foe.

"Wouldn't it be great if we could shut them out altogether?" he asked exultingly. "After the fuss they made about not wanting to play us, and the record they've made, if we could bar them from crossing our line—wouldn't it be immense?"

"'Dreams—idle dreams,'" quoted Dick with a smile. "I shouldn't ask anything better, but I'm afraid they're too strong for us. Why they came within an ace of beating Haskell the other day."

"That was on a fumble."

"I know, but fumbles count in football. No, if we beat them by a good score I'll be satisfied, even if they cross our line."

It was the day of the great game, a great game in the sense that Kentfield had made a record for herself in a remarkably short time under the skillful coaching of Mr. Martin and Mr. Spencer, and because she was to meet a foe who had despised her— meet a team that, hitherto had not considered our cadet heroes worthy of their steel. In a sense it was a triumph for Kentfield even before the game was started. As for Dick he was modestly proud.

There was a record-breaking crowd in attendance, for the word had gone around among lovers of football that Kentfield was putting up a great game, and the grandstands that in years past had held only a scattering throng, now overflowed.

"We'll be able to pay all our debts and close the season with a balance," exulted the manager and treasurer together.

"I'd rather win this game and lose every dollar!" cried Dick, as he ran to join his comrades on the gridiron.

Blue Hill was to kick off, and after the preliminary arrangements the pigskin was "teed" in midfield and there came a hush while each captain looked to see if his men were all placed.

"Are you ready?" came the call.

"Ready," answered Dick.

"Ready," answered Ford Haskell, the Blue Hill captain.

The whistle blew, and hardly had the echoes died away than there sounded the soul-stirring "ping" and the toe of Tod Kester's shoe dented the leather as the big centre sent the ball well into the territory of our friends.

"Now boys, back with it!" cried Dick. "Shove for all you are worth when it comes to a line up!"

Jake Weston caught the ball, and the speedy right end was down the field with it like a shot. He dodged several of the Blue Hill men, but at last Ned Buchanan, the husky right guard, got his arms around him, and Weston went down hard.

"Ready boys—come on," cried Dick, and this was the signal for a fake kick without any other word being given. They lined up and before the surprised Blue Hill team was aware of what was happening, and when their startled full-back had begun a retreat ready to catch the ball John Stiver had the pigskin, had passed it to Hal Foster and the latter smashed through the line for a ten yard gain.

"That's going some!" cried Innis Beeby when the scrimmage was over.

Indeed it was a good gain for that play, and Dick and his men rejoiced. Quickly they lined up again, and this time Dutton was sent smashing through between left guard and tackle. But this was not so successful, for the Blue Hill lads massed at that point, and blocked the advance after four yards had been covered.

But the ball had been advanced enough so that Dick felt he need not call for a punt, and this time he gave the signal for a play around right end. John Stiver got the ball and got into the play on the jump but to his own surprise and that of his comrades, he was almost nailed in his tracks by Lem Gordon, the husky left guard who broke through Innis Beeby.

Instead of a gain there was a loss of a few feet, and, seeing it, Dick felt his heart sink. Blue Hill had developed unexpected strength.

A kick was now necessary, and the ball was sent spinning into the enemy's territory. They ran it back a short distance, and then came their line up.

"Now, boys, see how we can hold 'em!" cried Dick cheerfully. "We'll have the pigskin in a couple of downs."

"Not much!" cried Captain Haskell, of the Blues.

Against the Kentfield line came smashing Rud Newton, the left half. He tried for a hole between Frank Rutley and Paul Drew at left tackle and guard respectively. Rutley held like a stone fence, but Paul, after a moment of opposition, gave way and Newton came smashing through. Dick and Hal Foster managed to nail him, however, but not before five yards were gained.

"You've got to hold better than that, boys!" called Dick, but they all knew it was Paul who had given way, and there was not one of them but what feared he would not hold out through the game. His recent illness was doubtless responsible.

Again Blue Hill tried a smashing play in the same place, hoping they had found a weak spot, but Dick and his men were ready, and Paul was supported to such advantage that not a foot was made.

There came a try for around the left end, but Tom Coleton and his colleagues were there ready to nab the man, and he actually ran back and was downed for a loss. Then came the inevitable kick, and Dick's side had the ball, practically where it had been in the first scrimmage.

"Do or die!" murmured our hero, and he called for some line-smashing plays. They were given with a will, but there was a defense that was well-nigh impregnable, and murmurs of astonishment began to go around among the spectators.

"They're as evenly matched teams as have ever played!" declared Coach Martin. "There may be no score."

"Oh, our boys have *got* to score!" cried Mr. Spencer.

Back and forth the game see-sawed, the ball most of the time, save when there was an exchange of kicks, being in the centre of the field. It was a kicking game, and Dick rejoiced that he had men who could be depended on to punt.

Again and again did the opposite sides hurl themselves against each other in the line, neither team being able to gain. Then a kick would be called for. This made it interesting for the spectators, but it was wearing on the players.

At last Dick, in desperation, decided on some sequence plays. These were three maneuvers to come one after the other at a certain signal, there being no word given for each individual play. Usually this was not done until the ball was within about twenty-five yards of the goal, when desperate work, to disconcert the opponents was necessary, but our hero thought he might now gain some ground in this way.

"We've got to do it! Pull together now!" called Dick. This meant that three plays, previously decided on were to come without further word from the quarter-back.

The plays were right half-back through right tackle, left tackle through right tackle and left half-back through right tackle, thus directing three smashing attacks in quick succession against the same place in the Blue Hill line.

The first attempt did not gain much, but when Frank Rutley came at the unfortunate Jean Trainor, who had just sustained one tremendous smash, there was a clean ten yards reeled off. Then, without a word being uttered, John Stiver jumped for the same breach on the next line up, and fifteen yards were gained.

Kentfield's supporters nearly went wild, for her boys were now within striking distance of the enemy's goal. But there was an enraged crowd of opponents to be reckoned with, for the Blue Hill cadets were half frenzied with the trick that had been played on them, and Dick knew he could not hope to work it again.

He called for an end run, and it seemed as if it would result in a good gain, but George Hall was downed before he had gone far. Then came a smash at the Blue Hill centre, and to the dismay of Dick, Paul Drew fumbled the ball. In an instant one of the Blue Hill players fell on it, and quickly booted it out of danger.

There was a groan, and Dick felt his heart sink. All their brilliant work in the sequence had gone for naught. The Blue Hill crowd went wild with delight.

"Line up!" called Dick grimly, and once more he began his line-smashing tactics. But there was no gain, and a kick was called for. Similarly the opponents of Kentfield could not advance the ball, and they punted. Then after some see-sawing work, time was called for the ending of the first half, with the ball on Blue Hill's forty-yard line. Neither side had scored.

"Well, what do you think of 'em?" asked Mr. Martin of Dick.

"Hard as nails," was the reply.

"I fancy they have the same opinion of you," said Mr. Spencer. "But I think you can get one touchdown the next half. They are tiring. Do you think you can risk another sequence play?"

"I believe so. I'll try it on the other side next time."

"I would, but wait until you're nearer their goal."

The rest period seemed all too short for the tired players, but they came out on the gridiron again leaping, laughing and shouting, though some showed the marks of the conflict.

There were shrill cries from many girls and women in the grandstands and Dick, giving a quick glance up saw Nellie Fordice, Mabel Hanford and some of their friends.

The second half began with a rush that meant business. Each side tried the line-smashing, but found it as before, and there was much kicking.

Blue Hill finally had the ball, and there was a moment's consultation before the signal was given. Then came a terrific smashing play at Paul Drew. Dick saw one of the Blue Hill players deliberately strike Paul in the stomach with his elbow. Poor Drew went down in a heap, and over him climbed the man with the ball, making a six yard gain before he could be stopped.

"A foul!" cried Dick, and reported to the umpire what he had witnessed. But that official had seen nothing, or at least said he had not.

"Watch 'em!" warned Dick to his players, while Paul had some wind pumped back into him.

"Can you play?" asked Mr. Martin.

"Yes—of course!" was the half-fierce reply.

Once more came a smashing attack at the unfortunate left guard. His opponents had discovered his weakness. Though he was not struck, the attack was so merciless that he could do nothing, and he had to be carried off the field, his weak condition being partly responsible, for his stomach still troubled him.

"Get in the game, Natron," called Dick, to the substitute guard, and then the Blue Hill attack was directed on the other side of the Kentfield line. But there Innis Beeby was ready for them, and he tackled his man with such fierceness that time had to be taken out to restore his half-scattered senses.

"They won't try any more slugging here," said the right guard grimly.

But Blue Hill was evidently "out for blood," and the slugging went on. The umpire saw it once, and ordered the offender out of the game.

All this while, however, the ball had been steadily advanced toward the Kentfield goal, and after Tom Coleton had been knocked out, giving Porter a chance to get back on his old position of left end, the advance was even faster.

Then, in one black and disheartening moment, came the fatal play. It was around Porter's end, in spite of the desperate effort Hal Foster made to tackle the man, the ball was touched down, and the goal kicked.

There were tears in the eyes of more than one Kentfield player, and Dick felt his heart sinking. But he grimly called on his men to respond, and for a time they had the ball in their enemy's territory.

Another of Dick's men was knocked out, and two of the Blue Hill players had to retire. The time was getting short, and Dick once more decided to use the sequence work, for with so many new cadets on the other side, he figured that they would not be prepared for them.

The plays were rattled through, and this time with such relentlessness that in a short time the ball was within ten yards of the Blue Hill goal.

"Touchdown! Touchdown!" came the imploring call from the Kentfield grandstands.

"Touchdown it shall be!" thought Dick fiercely. He sent Innis Beeby smashing through centre for three yards, and then, hoping Dutton could make the remaining distance, passed the ball to him.

Right into the line smashed the big right half-back, but someone tackled him with a fierceness that sent him unconscious to the ground, the ball rolled from his arms, and a moment later a Blue Hill man had it, and was racing down the field with all the speed left in him.

There was not a player to stop him, for all of Dick's team had been drawn close in, hoping for the touchdown, and before they were aware of what was happening the man with the ball was on the forty-yard line.

"Catch him! We've got to catch him!" yelled Dick. "It's another touchdown if we don't!"

After him sprinted every man on the Kentfield team, save Dutton who was still stretched on the ground, and then, straggling after their opponents, came the Blue Hills in scattered formation.

It was a foregone conclusion, for the Kentfield players were so wearied with their recent line-smashing attack that they could hardly run, and with tears in their eyes they saw the ball again touched down back of their goal posts. They had been so near to scoring, only to see their hopes dashed from them, and on what was nearly a fumble.

The goal was kicked and the score stood twelve to nothing against our friends. Dutton was revived, but was unable to resume play, and a substitute went in. There were only a few moments of the game left.

Desperately Dick called on his men for those last few minutes, and they did play to fierce advantage. There was some kicking, and when the Kentfields had the ball they rushed it down the field so fast that they were soon within striking distance of their opponents' goal.

Then fate, in the shape of the time whistle blew, and the contest was ended. Blue Hill had won.

CHAPTER XXIII

SORE HEARTS

"Dick, I'm so sorry."

It was Paul Drew who spoke, and he limped around the room where his chum sat staring gloomily out of the window into a mist of rain. The weather was in keeping with the hearts of the cadets of Kentfield academy.

"It was tough, wasn't it, Dick?"

"It was—very. I suppose I counted too much on winning that game. Others didn't seem so much to matter. But Blue Hill——"

"I know, Dick," and Paul spoke softly. "But they didn't play fair."

"That's what lots of the fellows say, and I saw you hit once. I've no doubt but what there was more slugging—but that doesn't excuse us for not winning."

"No, of course not, but——"

Paul was interrupted by a knock on the door. "Come in," called Dick, but there was no welcome in his tones.

"Say, old man, you act as though your best girl had sent back your letters unopened!" exclaimed Ray Dutton as he came in, wearing a bandage on his head, where he had been kicked in that last heart-breaking attack on the Blue Hill goal line. "Don't be so down and out about it. Kentfield has lost before, and lived through it."

"Yes, I suppose so," and Dick turned aside from the contemplation of the gloomy weather outside. "But it—hurts."

"Of course it does, but all is not lost yet. We have a chance for the championship."

"A mighty poor one."

"Well, it's a chance, isn't it? If we hadn't had so many men knocked out we could have won, even at that. Blue Hill made one touchdown against us by straight playing. We were about to do the same to her. Then they got one on a fumble. It was my fault for being so silly as to be knocked out, but——"

"It wasn't your fault at all!" cried Dick. "No one could have played better than you did. That whack on the head was enough to bowl anyone over."

"Yes, I guess it was," admitted Ray, as he gently felt of a lump the bandage covered.

"And the way they handled Paul was rotten," went on the captain.

"Oh, I'm not kicking," declared the plucky guard. "I'll be ready for 'em next time."

"I'm glad there is a next time," spoke Dick. "How do we stand, anyhow?"

"There are several games yet," said Dutton, "and we can win most of them easily. The only hard ones are with Mooretown and the next one with Blue Hill. That's the last, and we need to win that and the Mooretown contest to get the championship."

"It's a big contract," said the young millionaire with a sigh.

"Oh, brace up!" cried Dutton as cheerfully as he could. "Here come some of the fellows. Don't let 'em see you in the dumps, Dick."

Our hero tried to look cheerful, but it was hard work. Several of his players filed in. It was the day after the defeat by Blue Hill and there were sore bodies as well as sore hearts, for there had been more men knocked out in that desperate conflict than in any previous one. And, so said the senior cadets, there was no game ever played by Kentfield in all the years of her history that was more fiercely fought.

"Blue Hill has the best team in years," said Innis Beeby.

"So have we!" cried Jim Watkins.

"Granted, and we're going to be the champions," went on the big guard. "But it sure does make me sore to be licked after we practically made all our preparations to do Blue Hill."

Dick brightened up when he saw that he was not the only one who took the defeat to heart, and the talk drifted to the various incidents of the game. It was agreed that Blue Hill had not played exactly fair in a number of instances, but it was decided to keep quiet about this.

"They'll say we're soreheads if we kick," said Paul.

"I know one 'sorehead,'" remarked Ray with a grimace as he felt of his wound. "But wait until next time!"

The two coaches were disappointed but not discouraged. They had hoped, not only for their own prestige, but for the sake of the team, that Blue Hill would be defeated.

"But I'm glad there's another chance at them," remarked Mr. Martin grimly to his colleague.

"Yes, I fancy Blue Hill will have to bring along plenty of substitutes when we meet them again," and Mr. Spencer smiled.

"Oh, the next game is at their grounds, you know."

"Well, that isn't so good for our chances, but even at that I have no fear of the result. If we can get our boys into shape, and their injuries heal, I would be willing to stake a good sum on our side, if I were a betting man."

Porter was one of the disappointed ones, because he had lost a large sum of money on the result. He talked much about it, and even seemed inclined to blame Dick for the defeat.

"If he had let me go in earlier they wouldn't have gained so much on us," he said boastfully.

"Oh, get out!" cried Dutton in disgust. "Why, one of the biggest gains they made was around your end, and it resulted in a touchdown."

"Well, my foot slipped."

"And I guess the fellow's did who kicked me," said Ray grimly. "But don't make any cracks like that Porter. You're no better than the rest of us."

"I'm not saying I am, but I want to play from the start of the game next time."

He importuned Dick to this end, as soon as active practice was resumed, but Tom Coleton was again available and the captain did not feel like displacing him.

"He'd better look out, or I'll fix him!" threatened Porter to his crony Weston.

"What do you mean?"

"Dick Hamilton. He ought to let me play. I'll get square somehow."

"Oh, I wouldn't talk that way," said Weston weakly. He wanted to be loyal to his team, yet he was under obligations to Porter for he owed him a large sum of money. "You wouldn't do anything mean, would you?" he asked.

"Why doesn't Hamilton let me play then?" inquired Porter, not answering the question.

"I don't know. You may have a chance for one half of the Mooretown game."

"I want to play the whole game—not half, and if I get knocked out it's my fault. But I'd like to see the fellow try to do any funny business with me," and Porter shot out his jaw aggressively. He was quite a boxer in an amateur way.

"Well, don't do anything rash," cautioned his crony, but Porter walked off, muttering to himself.

Gradually the soreness and stiffness of the players wore off toward the end of the week and they were practicing with their usual vim. Though many had been on the hospital list, almost the entire Varsity was available for a game the next Saturday, when one of the league contests was played with Ralston Academy. Kentfield won easily, and further clinched her chances for being the champion. But the hardest games—those of Blue Hill and Mooretown were yet to come.

Of Mooretown, Dick had no fear as to the result, but Blue Hill was another matter. Still he strengthened his heart when he saw his men in vigorous practice.

"They certainly are a great team!" he exulted, "and they are as hard as nails."

Even in the gloom of defeat and in the preparation for gridiron battles yet to come, Dick had not forgotten his father's troubles. He kept in communication with Mr. Hamilton, and learned that matters were temporarily at a standstill.

"They can't get the controlling lot of stock from Mr. Duncaster, and neither can I," wrote Dick's father. "So matters stand. But I have a new plan. I am coming to Kentfield soon, and I'll see that obstinate gentleman myself."

"Dad coming here!" cried Dick in delight as he read the letter to Paul. "I hope he's in time for the Mooretown game."

CHAPTER XXIV

TREACHERY

Mr. Hamilton arrived at Kentfield the day before the game with Mooretown. Dick welcomed his parent enthusiastically, and introduced him to all his chums, with whom the millionaire was soon on friendly terms.

"You'll have a chance to see us play, dad!" cried the captain. "You'll go Mooretown with us; won't you?"

"To see you beaten?" asked Mr. Hamilton quizzically.

"Not much! We'll wipe up the gridiron with them!" cried Ray Dutton. "We've got to, if we want that loving cup," he added with a laugh, "and Blue Hill, too."

"Well, I guess I'll come," assented Dick's father. "But I have some business to transact first."

"I'm afraid you won't transact much of it," spoke Dick in a low voice. "Mr. Duncaster is very obstinate."

"How are you going to Mooretown?" inquired Mr. Hamilton.

"By special train. Our manager has arranged for one. I did think of autos, but the roads are pretty poor and then we want to take a big crowd with us to 'root' for a win. So we'll go by train."

"Then I'll come along. Now tell me about this Mr. Duncaster," and Dick proceeded to do so, detailing his own visit, and that of Mr. Larabee.

"Hum! A hard man to do business with. Still I've got to try, for it means a lot to me," and Mr. Hamilton sighed. Dick noticed with regret that his father's face was much more wrinkled than it had been, and the gray hairs were more numerous.

"The strain is telling on him," mused the lad. "I wonder what would happen if he lost all his money—and if I lost mine," for of late Dick had transferred most of his funds to his father, to use in the electric road deal. In fact most of the Hamilton fortune was now tied up in that line.

"But I guess dad will make out," concluded our hero. "He has been in tight places before, and has always pulled through."

Mr. Hamilton set off to see Enos Duncaster, and Dick made his father promise to take dinner with him that night at the Sacred Pig where an impromptu spread had been arranged in honor of the visit of the millionaire. Major Webster Colonel Masterly, and several of the academy faculty had promised to attend.

"It won't be much on the 'eat' line for you fellows and me," Dick had warned them, "we can't break training until after we have wiped out the disgrace of the Blue Hill defeat, and that won't be for two weeks. Then we'll have a feast that is a feast."

"Good!" cried Innis Beeby for he was fond of feasts, and suffered under the rigorous football regime.

Dick was waiting for his father's return from Mr. Duncaster's house that evening, sitting in his room trying to study. He was not making much headway for he was thinking of many things—of the game on the morrow—of the one with Blue Hill, and of what success his father would meet with. Paul Drew was out at a society meeting.

There came a knock on the door, a timid hesitating sort of a knock, and Dick, wondering who it could be, called out:

"Come in!"

Sam Porter entered, first looking around the apartment to see that Dick's roommate was not present.

"Are you busy, Hamilton?" he asked, and there was that in his voice that caused Dick to wonder at him. There was a thickness and a sort of leering familiarity that was unusual.

"No, I'm not busy. Come in and make yourself comfortable. There's an easy chair," and Dick knocked a pile of books from one to make room for his visitor.

"I want to ask a favor of you, Hamilton, and I want you to grant it—understand?" and Porter looked sharply at the captain. "I want you to promise."

"I can't promise, until I hear what it is," said the young millionaire good-naturedly.

"Yes you can—if you want to—un'stand?" Sam Porter leaned forward.

"You want to grant me this favor—un'stand," went on Porter, "or you'll be sorry. Sorry, see?"

"What is it?" asked Dick, trying not to show the disgust he felt.

"I want to play in that Mooretown game to-morrow—play full game—un'stand? I don't want to sit on side lines like some poor Indian wrapped up in a blanket—I want to go in from start an' wallop them fellers. Un'stand? I want to play. You can put me in as well as not. Will you? It's favor, Ham, an' if you don't do it, you'll be sorry!"

"Why?" asked Dick, for there was a vague threat in the tones of his caller.

"Well, nev' min'. Will you let me play?"

Porter was not himself. Dick had never seen him thus, and he feared lest some of the teachers discover his condition. He thought it best to temporize with him.

"I'll see what I can do," he promised good-naturedly. "Come and see me in the morning. You'd better go to bed now."

"Go to bed?" and Porter's voice rose. "Why, wha's matter me? Ain't I a'right?"

"Yes, but if you are to play to-morrow you'll need a rest. See me in the morning."

"All right. I'll go. But if I can't play whole game you be sorry, Ham. You're good feller—you let me play—be sorry if you don't—tha's all," and Porter lurched from the room, while Dick shook his head sorrowfully.

Mr. Hamilton came up to Dick's room about an hour later. It needed but a look at his face to see that his errand had proven a failure.

"Well?" asked Dick, but he knew what the answer would be.

"Mr. Duncaster wouldn't even talk to me when he learned what my object was," said the millionaire wearily. "I guess we can't do anything with him, Dick. But never mind," he added more brightly, "I can try another scheme. They haven't got us beaten yet, Dick, my boy!"

Dick put his father up in an apartment in the Sacred Pig after the little banquet. It was a gay affair in spite of the millionaire's disappointment, and the boys voted him a brick.

Porter approached the captain the next morning. He did not seem at all ashamed of his condition of yesterday.

"Well, Hamilton, am I to play?" was the somewhat sharp question.

"You'll have to take your chances with the other subs," was the young captain's answer. "I can't make any changes in the Varsity now. I may after the first half, if we find Mooretown easy enough."

"Yes, that's it!" sneered Porter. "You'll only put me in on the easy games. I won't stand for it. Either I play the full game, or off comes my suit for the season."

"You can please yourself about that," and Dick turned aside.

"You'll be sorry for this!" muttered Porter, as he walked away.

The last arrangements had been made, the team and substitutes surrounded by the crowd of students who could not go to Mooretown, had been cheered again and again, and Grit had been decorated as a mascot.

The crowd which was to accompany the players on the special train had all gathered, and the march to the depot was begun. Mr. Hamilton was with Dick.

"Humph! Our special hasn't pulled in yet," observed Manager Hatfield when the station was reached, and there were no cars in waiting "That's funny. The agent said it would be surely here ready for us. I'll ask him about it."

Dick was standing near the manager when he questioned the station master. That official seemed greatly surprised at the crowd of players and spectators.

"Your special train?" he exclaimed. "Why you countermanded the order for it. The game was off, I understood, so I sent the engine and cars back."

"Sent them back!" cried Dick. "How was that?"

"Why, I had them all here, and the engineer had steam up, waiting for you. About an hour ago one of your students came down here and said Mooretown had cancelled the game, and that you weren't going to play. So, as I didn't want the special standing here in the way of the regular trains, I sent it back to the yard."

"Can we get it again?" asked Hatfield, wondering what had happened.

"Not inside of several hours."

"What sort of a student told you we didn't want it?" asked Dick, excitedly.

"A tall lad, rather stout, and with quite a good color—you know—sort of beefy."

"Porter!" whispered Dick, involuntarily, and several heard him.

"The special has been sent back, we can't get a train in several hours, and we're due at Mooretown at two o'clock," spoke the manager. "They'll claim the game by forfeit if we don't show up, and then——"

"Good-bye to our chances for the championship," put in Beeby gloomily.

"There's been treachery here," murmured Dick, as he gazed at the blank faces of his companions. "Treachery! This is what Sam Porter meant when he said I'd be sorry."

CHAPTER XXV

A DESPERATE RACE

For a few moments the surprise of the cadets was such that they could think of nothing to do. It seemed almost impossible that their plans should be defeated by such a simple means, yet such was the case. A look down the empty tracks showed not a sign of their special train, and further appeals to the agent only confirmed what he had first said.

"It's no use, boys," he declared. "That special has been sent back and it will take a long time to get it again, even if I could. The train dispatcher made a certain schedule for it, and once that is busted it's hard to get it in shape again."

"Isn't there a regular train they can take?" asked Mr. Hamilton.

"Not for three hours."

"And that will be too late," said Paul dismally.

"Whew!" whistled George Hall. "This is tough! Let's wire Mooretown and tell them what happened. They'll call the game off I'm sure, and not make it a forfeit for us."

"What good would it do if they did?" asked Jim Watkins. "There are only two more games for us to play in the championship series. This one with Mooretown and the one next Saturday with Blue Hill. This is our only chance, and if we can't take it we won't get another one at Mooretown, as they break training to-day, after this contest. No boys, it's all up with Kentfield's chance at the trophy, I reckon."

There was silence for a moment, but the cadets were doing some hard thinking.

"That cad Porter!" exclaimed Innis Beeby. "What could have induced him to play such a contemptible trick?"

"I suppose because I wouldn't promise to let him go in for the full game to-day," replied Dick reluctantly.

"Are you sure it was Porter?" inquired Paul.

"He's about the only one who is capable of such a thing as this," said Innis, looking at Weston.

"I'm going to make sure," spoke Dick, and he inquired particularly of the agent as to the appearance of the cadet who had given the false information about there being no need of the special train. The detailed description left no room for doubt. It was Porter.

"And, now I come to think of it, the young man laughed as he was going away, after he heard me give the engineer of the special the orders that he wouldn't be needed," said the station agent.

"He laughed; eh?" repeated Dick.

"Yes, and I think he said something about a joke, but I can't be sure. Anyhow I thought it was sort of funny to hear him chuckle when he was walking away, for I know how set you boys are on football, and I reckoned you'd be sorry if a game was cancelled. But I had other things to think of, getting the trains on their regular schedule after the special was out of the way, so I didn't pay much attention."

"Well, Porter has put us in bad," declared Ray Dutton. "The sneak! I wish I had him here now."

Several glances were turned in the direction of the crony of Porter, as if he might know something of him. Weston flushed uneasily, but he rose to the situation.

"Fellows," he said earnestly, "I hope you don't think that I had any hand in this. Porter and I have been thick, I know, but of late he hasn't had so much to do with me. But, on my honor, I never knew a thing about this. He never hinted it to me, or if he had I hope you will believe me when I say that I wouldn't have stood for it, and that I'd have told Hamilton right away, so his mean plan could have been stopped. I hope you believe me."

"Of course we do, Weston," said Dick. "I'm afraid Porter hasn't been himself lately. But let's forget about that now. The thing to do is to consider how we are going to get to Mooretown."

"How can we, without a train available?" asked Beeby.

"I don't know—I'm going to think," declared the captain with a brave effort to keep cheerful against heavy odds.

"Suppose you let me try," suggested Mr. Hamilton. "I know some of the higher railroad officials, and if I telegraph them they may be able to get a special back here in time for you to play."

The boys brightened up at this, and the millionaire wrote several messages which the agent clicked off to headquarters. There was barely time, if a special arrived inside of half an hour, for the cadets to get to Mooretown in season to play the game, but it was a small margin.

"If we had carriages enough we could drive," said Hal Foster. "The wagon road to Mooretown is shorter than the railroad line."

"We never could do it in time," objected Frank Rutley.

At this moment the agent came out from the office with several telegrams in his hand.

"I'm sorry," he announced, "but they say at headquarters, Mr. Hamilton, that they'd like to oblige you and the boys, but two hours is the shortest time in which they can get the special in shape again. No engineer is available."

Once more dull hopelessness fell upon the boys. Dick was almost in despair. He saw all his plans of being captain of a championship football team being dashed to the ground. It was a bitter blow.

The two coaches, likewise, were much disappointed, for it would be not a little to their credit to have whipped into first class shape a team that, the season before, was the tail-ender of the military colleges.

The young captain was pacing up and down the depot platform. His companions left him alone for a space for they knew how he felt.

"Well," began Dick after a pause, "I guess——"

He did not finish the sentence, but stood in a listening attitude. From down the road there came a steady hum and roar that told of some approaching vehicles.

"Automobiles," remarked Paul Drew. "If we had enough of them——"

An instant later there swung into view around the bend in the road four big auto trucks, new ones, each in charge of a man. The trucks were powerful ones, designed to carry heavy loads a long distance and they glistened with new paint, while in gold letters on their sides was the name of a business firm in a large city just beyond Mooretown.

At the sight of these—of their ample capacity—large enough to take the team and the crowd with them, Dick's heart gave a bound. He made up his mind instantly.

"Fellows!" he cried, "if those men will hire me those trucks we'll play Mooretown yet. I'm going to see!"

"Hurray!" cried George Hall, and Mr. Hamilton smiled in a gratified way at the quick wit of his son.

"I say!" cried the young millionaire, stepping out in front of the first truck and holding up his hand, "will you do us a favor?"

"What's this—a—hold up?" asked the man good-naturedly, as he jammed on the brakes.

"Yes, we're held up—our special has gone—we've got to get to Mooretown soon or we forfeit the championship game. Will you take us in those trucks? I'll pay you well, and stand for all damage. Will you?"

His voice was eager, and the man, who had been a boy himself once, and fond of sport, was visibly impressed.

"I'd like to oblige you," he said slowly, "but I don't know as I can. You see I'm in charge of these four trucks. I work for the auto firm that built them, and the flour company in Denville that purchased them made an agreement that before they would accept them, the machines must be run from the factory to their place. That's what I and my men are doing now. The flour concern wanted to test the running gear, and it will be a good test all right."

"It will be a better test with a load of us fellows in," said Dick with ready wit.

"I suppose so," admitted the man, scratching his head, "but I don't know as the flour firm would like it. There might be some damage, and——"

"I'll stand for it!" put in Mr. Hamilton quickly. "I'm Mortimer Hamilton, of Hamilton Corners."

Though he spoke quietly his words had an instant effect for the man had evidently heard of the millionaire.

"Is that so?" asked the chief auto driver quickly. "I know you. I own two shares of stock in your electric road. Simpson is my name—Ruddy Simpson. I hope the rumors that the road is going to fail aren't true, Mr. Hamilton."

"The road will never fail, if I have to sink in it every dollar I own!" cried Mr. Hamilton. "But we've got other business in hand now. Can you take these boys to the game?"

"I'll do it!" suddenly cried Mr. Simpson. "I'll take a chance. Hop in boys, and I'll get you there on time if the gasolene holds out. We've got to pass through Mooretown to Denville. Hop in!"

"Hurrah!" cried the now hopeful cadets, and they piled into the four big trucks. They had to stand up, and there was considerable crowding, but they did not mind this, and there was room for all.

"Now for the game!" cried Dick as the ponderous machines started off, the station agent waving a farewell.

"I guess this will put a spoke in Porter's wheel," murmured Beeby. "He'll feel sick to think that we got to the game after his mean trick."

"We're not there yet," remarked Dick a bit dubiously, for he knew the eccentricities of autos. "We've got to make pretty good time, and there are several hills to climb."

"Don't let them hills worry you," said Mr. Simpson. "I helped build these trucks, and I know what they can do. We'll take any hill you can give us, with a heavier load than this on. Only, of course, we haven't an awful lot of speed. But I'll push them to the limit. Turn on all you can!" he called back to the three men.

"Sure!" they shouted in reply, and the motors hummed and throbbed under the strain.

For the first few miles the roads were good, and speedy time was made, so that Dick ceased some of his worry lest they arrive too late. Then a sandy stretch was encountered, and the motors whined out a protest, but they kept on.

"Think you can do it?" asked the captain of the man in charge. Dick and the team and substitutes, together with his father, were in the first machine.

"Oh, we'll do it," was the reply, and Mr. Simpson's voice had a confidence he did not altogether feel. It was no small responsibility, for it was a desperate race against the fleeting minutes and hours.

After the sand, came a good piece of highway, and then a stiff hill, but the trucks made it safely and at fair speed.

"We'll do it!" announced Mr. Simpson after about two hours. "There's one long hill now after this one we're climbing and then we can coast down into Mooretown."

"Good!" cried Dick, and he felt some of the strain of anxiety leaving him.

A few minutes later, when the foremost auto had reached the crest of the rise, the driver of the truck containing Dick and the team remarked, as he pointed ahead:

"There's Mooretown, but you can't see the cadet football field yet."

"Oh, I guess they'll be there expecting us," replied the young captain.

Down the other side of the long slope started the first truck, the others following in procession.

"Well, we did better than I expected we would," remarked Mr. Simpson. "These trucks——"

He stopped suddenly, as a sharp jar and crash came from somewhere in the mechanism of the machinery. The brakes had been set as the descent was begun, and the car had been traveling slowly, but now a sudden increase in speed was noticed.

"What's the matter?" asked Mr. Hamilton quickly.

"Aren't we going a bit too fast down hill?" inquired Mr. Martin.

The driver shut his lips with a grim tightening. He yanked back on the brake handle with all his force. Then a startled look came over his face.

"The brake rod is broken!" he cried.

Gathering speed the ponderous truck, with its load of humanity—the cadet football team shot down hill, bumping over stones and hollows, swerving from side to side, the steering wheel making the firm hands of the driver tremble.

"Haven't you got two brakes?" gasped Dick.

"Yes—got the foot on one—she won't hold her with this load," was the panting answer.

"Can't we jump out before it goes any faster?" asked Hal Foster.

"Stay where you are!" fairly shouted the man. "Maybe I can guide her down."

147 | P a g e

He was tooting the horn frantically to warn possible approaching vehicles that his was out of control. Fortunately the hill was straight, and a level stretch at the bottom gave promise of a long coast that might check the awful speed the car would have when it reached the foot of the declivity.

Faster and faster went the runaway truck, and now from behind came the frantic calls of the other cadets who realized the danger to their football team. And there was grave danger—danger that could not be avoided, for Simpson, yanking again and again on the brake lever, only made more certain that it would not work, and the foot brake was pitifully inadequate to check the now rushing vehicle.

CHAPTER XXVI

ANOTHER GAME

There was silence for a time among the cadets of the football team—silence broken only by the whirr and hum of the machinery as it ran free, for the gasolene had been shut off. Under the big tires crunched the small stones and gravel of the road.

"Can't you start the motor and hold her back on the reverse?" shouted Dick above the noise.

Simpson shook his head.

"I'd rip her all to pieces if I did," he answered. "Queer about that brake rod snapping. That's not in my department, but I'd like to get hold of the man that inspected and tested it," he added grimly. "I'd break him!"

Dick looked into the faces of his chums. There was a quiet, strained look in all of them, but none of them showed craven fear. He glanced at his father, and Mr. Hamilton smiled at his son.

"I guess we won't be behind hand now," he said.

"No," and Dick shook his head. Then he glanced over the side of the truck and noted how the trees were slipping by. They were going at ever-increasing speed.

Luckily they met no other vehicles on the hill, or there might have been trouble. The auto drivers in the rear, finding they could do nothing were keeping up as close as they could, to render any assistance if possible.

It was well that the speeding truck was strongly and ponderously made, and that it was hung low, otherwise it would have toppled over. As it was they all swayed from side to side dangerously, tossing the occupants against one another.

"Good practice for the coming game," remarked Dutton.

"I hope it doesn't take their nerve," said Mr. Martin in a low voice to his colleague. "This may have a fearful effect."

"Their nerves are good," declared the Princeton coach, "but I wish this was over. There's a good bit yet to go, and we'll travel faster at the end, for the hill is steeper there."

Mr. Martin silently nodded, and then looked ahead. As he did so he could not refrain from a startled cry, for the hill took a sudden, steep dip, and it seemed impossible for any auto not under control to make it successfully.

Before any one could do anything, had it been possible, the car was at the dangerous descent. Simpson drew in his breath sharply and grasped the steering wheel with firmer grip.

"Whew!" whistled Paul Drew. "This is awful!"

Dick said nothing, but he moved up closer to his father. Fear was clutching his heart, for he dreaded lest that all be killed.

"This is about the end!" gasped the driver, as the steeper part of the hill came to an end. "The worst is over."

The cadets could now look ahead, and see a level stretch. They were beginning to breathe easier.

"Once I'm on that I'll be all right," went on the driver. He reached it a moment later, but the speed of the ponderous car was not checked much. It had too great momentum.

Suddenly Dick gave a cry of fear, and pointed forward. They all saw it at the same time. Three hundred feet away was a narrow bridge and at that moment there appeared on it, turning in from a side road, a man driving a team of horses attached to a light carriage. And, as the cadets looked, the horses seemed possessed with sudden fright at the view of the oncoming auto. They reared, and the driver had all he could do to hold them in.

Then one animal, worse than its mate, kicked over the traces and, coming down, got tangled in the harness. It fell heavily, right in the centre of the bridge, dragging down its mate. The man leaped out to go to the heads of the horses, and, as he saw the approaching auto he held up his hand and shouted a warning.

"Stop! Stop!" he cried.

"I can't!" yelled back Simpson. "Cut the harness! Push the horses off the bridge!"

The man was working frantically. Simpson gave a last desperate yank on the brake lever. It was still out of commission, as he knew it would be. There seemed to be no escape from the impending crash which might mean death for a number of them.

"I'm going to jump!" cried George Hall, worming his way to the rear of the truck, which was going almost as fast as when on the hill.

"Don't you do it!" cried Dick, with all the energy he possessed. "Here, Simpson, turn into that hayfield! Make for the stack! Run the auto into it! That will stop us without damage!"

"By gasolene! I believe you're right!" yelled the driver. "I'll do it. It's our only hope."

"But the fence! The fence!" shouted Paul. "We'll smash into it!" for a rail fence shut off from the road the field at which Dick had pointed.

"That fence!" yelled Simpson in supreme contempt. "I'll smash it into kindling wood! Hold fast everybody! Here we go!"

A moment later he had swung the car toward the hayfield. Fortunately it was on a level with the road, or the front part of the auto would never have sustained the shock. Through the fence the ponderous machine crashed as if it were paper. The next instant the big car plowed straight into a big stack of hay.

Like so many rubber balls, the football players were thrown forward against one another, and Dick and the two coaches were tossed out into the fragrant timothy.

Then a cheer burst from the other cadets in the three following trucks which had come to a stop. For they saw that their comrades were safe. The man on the bridge had succeeded in disentangling his horses and they were now quiet.

Simpson leaped from his seat, which he had managed to maintain, and looked under the truck.

"I knew it!" he cried. "Brake rod busted. Oh, if I had the man who made that!"

"Can we go on?" asked Dick anxiously as he picked himself up from the hay.

"Wouldn't dare to without this brake rod being fixed" replied the driver. "There are more hills."

"Here, you football fellows get in one of these other trucks. We'll pile out and walk to the grounds—it's not far," called Percy Haddon.

"That's the stuff!" shouted Manager Hatfield. "We haven't any too much time. Are you boys all right?"

"Sure," answered Paul with a laugh. "We're ready to play the game of our lives."

"That's right!" came in a chorus from the others. Now that the strain was over there was a bit of hysterical feeling, but it soon passed away.

Little time was lost in making the transfer. The football team and the substitutes got in one of the other trucks and were soon being whizzed off to the grounds. The other two trucks, containing as many of the remaining cadets as could squeeze into them, pressed on, and only a few had to walk the remaining distance.

Simpson backed his truck out of the hayfield which had practically saved a number of lives that day. Then the driver began work at repairing the brake rod, his companions promising to return for him when they had taken the cadets to the grounds.

Nor would Simpson accept any pay for the services he had rendered that day.

"I've got stock in your road, Mr. Hamilton," he said, "though it is only two shares. This was a good test of the trucks, and I'm glad only a brake rod busted. It was better to happen now than after I had delivered 'em. I'm satisfied."

The Mooretown cadets were becoming anxious about the non-appearance of their opponents, for the hour for the game was fast approaching, when Dick and his players came running out on the gridiron. They were greeted with a rousing cheer, for, though the rules called for the forfeiting of a contest to the non-appearing team, the Mooretown cadets were true sportsmen and hated to take this advantage.

"Jove! But I'm glad you fellows came!" cried the Mooretown captain as he wrung Dick's hand. "We were horribly afraid you wouldn't show up. What was the matter? I thought you were coming by special train."

"We were, but there was a mix-up and we had to charter these autos. But we're here and we're going to beat you!"

"Yes, you are!" and the home captain laughed. "Well, I'll show you the dressing rooms. We've got a smashing big crowd here to-day and the weather is just right. It would have been a shame to disappoint 'em."

"Well, it's too bad to have 'em see you defeated, but it can't be helped," said Dick with mocking seriousness and they both laughed. The fright of the dangerous ride was fast passing away from all of the Kentfield team.

They were soon in their suits and out on the gridiron practicing. Meanwhile the Mooretown lads were at work with the ball, and the Kentfield coaches were critically sizing them up.

"Not nearly as fast as our lads," declared Mr. Martin.

"That's right. I don't expect a walkover, but there ought to be no question as to who is going to win—unless this auto affair has got on the nerves of our lads."

The crowd continued to arrive. The grandstands were like some gorgeous sunset in appearance, with the hats of the pretty girls, and the waving of flags and banners. Cheers and songs, made music in keeping with the day.

"Line-up!" came the cry, and when the whistle blew, and the ball was kicked off, twenty-two figures clad in earth-stained suits made a mad dash for each other. The game was on.

From the time of the first scrimmage Dick knew that his team had the contest safe, for one smashing through the line of Mooretown told the story. The men had over-trained and had gone "stale." On the other hand the Kentfield lads were as fresh as the proverbial daisies.

"Take her along for a touchdown, boys!" ordered the captain, and down the field the ball was worked in a steady succession of rushes. In vain did Mooretown try to stem the tide against them. Once, when their goal line was almost reached, they did brace, and Dick began to plan a trick play. But it was not needed, for the next moment Dutton was shoved over for the touchdown, and the crowd of Kentfield students went wild with delight. The goal was kicked easily, and then began the hammer and tongs work again.

Once again that half Kentfield made a touchdown, not as easily as at first, for Mooretown had waxed desperate, but it was made. Not that it was all "pie" to quote Dick, but they had the "measure" of their opponents, and they began to see the championship looming clearly before them.

Twelve to nothing was the score in favor of Kentfield at the end of the first half, which came to a close with the ball once more almost over the Mooretown line.

There were sore hearts among the players on the home team, and Dick and his lads knew just how their opponents felt, but it was a fair game, with no quarter and it was the fortunes of war.

"I'm afraid you're going to make good," said the Mooretown captain to the young millionaire, as the second half started.

"We've just *got* to," answered Dick. "We want that gold cup."

Hammering away again, the Kentfield lads advanced the ball. Mooretown got it on a fumble once, and did some pretty work in punting, but it was of no avail. Again they had the pigskin because of the penalty inflicted on a too eager Kentfield player, and they made a desperate try for a field goal, but it fell short.

After that there was no more danger to our friends, and they kept the ball advancing by steady rushes, or, to rest his men, Dick would call for a forward pass. Again and yet again was the Mooretown goal line crossed, amid the frantic cheers of the Kentfield contingent, and when the final whistle blew the score was twenty-nine to nothing.

"Victory!" cried Dick in exultation, as he hugged as many of his players as he could. "Now for Blue Hill next Saturday and we'll have such a feast as never was at Kentfield before!"

CHAPTER XXVII

DICK IS SUMMONED

The Kentfield cadets accepted the invitation of their late opponents, to stay and see them break training.

"As long as we didn't have a chance at the championship I'm glad you fellows have," confided Captain Russell of Mooretown to Dick. "Of course we'd have liked to have beaten you chaps, but I guess we over-trained. We haven't any regular coaches, and we did the best we could."

"You sure did," assented Dick heartily. "It's too bad you went back. You were fine early in the season."

"I know it, and that shows that it pays to have regular coaches who know their business. How in the world did you fellows manage to get Martin and Spencer?"

"Oh, we worked it by a forward pass," replied the young millionaire with a laugh.

There was jolly fun at Mooretown that night, in spite of the defeat. The team burned their suits at a big bonfire, and danced around the blaze like Indians, singing college songs and cheering their opponents who, in turn shouted for their plucky but unfortunate enemies.

Then came a long and rather dreary ride back to Kentfield in a way-train that stopped at every station. But the boys enlivened the trip by songs and cheers so that they were not very lonesome.

"Well Dick, I must get back in the morning," said Mr. Hamilton to his son when they said good-night in Dick's room.

"You won't try to see Duncaster again?"

"No, it would be of little use. He is evidently set in his ways. My only hope is that he doesn't turn over to the other side. If he does——"

The millionaire paused.

"Well?" asked Dick suggestively.

"The Hamilton fortune will be a thing of the past, son."

"As bad as that?"

Mr. Hamilton nodded.

"But I'm not going to give up," he declared. "I have some other irons in the fire, and I may be able to forge them to the shape I want. It's going to be hard work, though, and it would be much easier if I had the Duncaster stock. By the way, you say that Porter chap, whose father is working against us, attends here?"

"Yes, but I fancy he won't after to-morrow," said Dick significantly.

He was right. Sam Porter's room was vacant the next day, and he left no word of where he had gone. He knew his trick had been discovered, and that it had gone for naught.

Several days later he sent a note to his former crony Weston, asking to see him, but Weston refused.

"I was his friend once," he said to Dick, "but I'm done with him now. I'm for the football team first, last and forever!"

"And you're one of our best players!" exclaimed the young captain heartily, for he appreciated what it meant to break with Porter.

Football matters at Kentfield were now drawing to a close. There was but one more game to play—that of Blue Hill, but in the eyes of the cadets it was the most important of the season because of what the outcome carried with it. There was a tie for the championship between our hero's football eleven and that of the academy which had sent the insulting letter that resulted in such a change of policy.

"Get ready for the last week of practice," ordered Coach Martin, on the Monday following the Mooretown game. "It's going to be hard, too, but I don't want any one to over-train. Take it a bit easy when you find yourself tiring."

"Yes, we want you in the pink of perfection Saturday," added Mr. Spencer.

There followed days of the most careful preparation. It was like getting ready for the final great battle between two rival armies. Football suits were looked to, for a rip in a jacket or a sweater might spoil a play at a critical point. The lads replaced the worn cleats on their shoes, that they might brace themselves when the Blue Hill players hurled themselves at the Kentfield line.

As for their physical condition, the cadets were looked over by the trainers and coaches as if they were race horses. Tender ankles were carefully treated and bandaged. Sprains were rubbed in the most scientific manner, and did any one complain of a little indisposition the coaches were up in alarm.

And the boys were in the "pink of condition." Never had they felt finer nor more able to do battle for the championship. Never were they more confident, for, somehow, Dick had talked them into the firm belief that they were going to win.

As for our hero, he had a worry that he kept to himself, and, now that his father had returned to Hamilton Corners, the lad let it prey on his mind even more than he had when the millionaire was at the academy.

"Our fortune in danger," mused Dick. "That sure is tough luck. Not that money is everything, or really much in this world. But, after you've gotten used to having it, I guess it's hard to spin along without it. But perhaps it won't be so bad as dad fears. I would certainly hate to give up my steam yacht, and I may have to leave Kentfield. Whew! That would pull a lot!" and he sat staring in moody silence at the walls of his tastefully decorated room.

There was a movement at Dick's feet and Grit half arose to poke his cold nose into his master's listless hand. The lad started.

"Grit, old boy!" he murmured and the animal whined in delight. "Whatever happens they can't take you from me," went on the young millionaire. "But there's Rex. Maybe I can't afford to keep a horse. Oh, but I'd hate to part with him!"

He could not keep back just a suspicion of tears from his eyes, as he stroked the short ears of the bulldog, who seemed to know that something was amiss.

"Oh, well, what's the use of crying over spilled milk before you come to the bridge!" Dick exclaimed at length. "I'm not going to worry until it's time; and that isn't yet. Guess I'll go for a canter on Rex. That will clear the cobwebs away."

He was soon galloping over the country, glad to be alone for a little while to think over the problems that were bothering him. As the noble animal galloped along around the lake path, and Dick felt the cool November wind on his cheeks, somehow there came to him a feeling of peace.

"After all, it may come out right," he whispered as he patted the neck of the horse. "And I'm going to have one more try at Duncaster. I won't undertake to see him. I'll write him a letter and explain some things he doesn't understand. Maybe it will just pull him the right way."

The thought was an inspiration to him, and he turned Rex about and galloped to the stables.

"Well, what's all the correspondence about Dick?" asked Paul that evening, as his chum was busily scratching away in their room. "I thought you answered Miss Hanford's last letter yesterday."

"Humph! Seems to me you've been doing something in the way of writing letters yourself. But this is business. I'm making a last appeal to Duncaster."

Dick was not very hopeful as he mailed the epistle to Hardvale.

It was the day of the Blue Hill Game, and final practice, save for a little "warm-up" on the gridiron, just before time should be called, had been held. The coaches had issued their last instructions, Dick had given his men a little talk, and all that could be done had been done.

"It's do or die now," grimly remarked the young captain. "We're fit to the minute."

"Have you heard from Duncaster?" asked Paul.

"No, and I don't expect to. He'll keep the stock I expect, or trade it to the Porter crowd. It was a slim chance, but it didn't make good."

"Well," remarked Paul, a little later, when Dick had been nervously pacing about the room. "I suppose we might as well go out on the gridiron."

"It's a bit early," objected Dick. "The Blue Hill crowd won't be here for an hour yet."

There came a knock on the door, and Toots stood there saluting between the strains of "Marching Through Georgia."

"Telegram for you, Mr. Hamilton—it came collect," announced the janitor.

"Humph. Can't be from dad, he always pays his messages," remarked Dick, as he handed over the money, and tore open the envelope. When he had read the few words he gave a gasp of astonishment.

"What's the matter?" asked Paul quickly. "Bad news."

"No. Good!" cried Dick. "Listen. This is from Mr. Duncaster—no wonder he sent it collect. He says: 'Have your letter. I will grant your request and sell you the stock. Come and see me at once, as I am leaving for Europe for my health. I go to-night.'"

"Then you'd better hustle out to Hardvale!" cried Paul. "Hurray! That's great."

Slowly Dick crushed the telegram in his hand.

"I can't go," he said slowly.

"Why not?"

"I haven't time to go out there and get back to play the game—and—I'm going to play the game!"

CHAPTER XXVIII

"LINE UP!"

Paul, looked at Dick Hamilton with something a little short of open-mouthed wonder. He could not understand him. He realized the vital necessity of the Hamilton forces getting control of the trolley stock that Mr. Duncaster held. Now, when the opportunity offered, Dick calmly turned it down.

"Do you know what you're saying, Dick?" asked his roommate. "This is the only chance you'll have—perhaps to save your father's fortune."

"I know it."

"And you're not going?"

"What? And desert the team in the face of the biggest game of the year? I guess not. Dad wouldn't want me to."

"Some one can play in your place—perhaps for half the game. You could go out in an auto and back in a short time."

"Of course I might, but I'm not going to," and the young millionaire, who might not be a lad of wealth much longer, calmly looked to see if his canvas jacket needed any last attention. "If I went out there it would take some time to arrange about the transfer of the stock, and I never could get back in season to play the game. Besides I want to start off with the boys from the first kick against Blue Hill."

"I don't blame you—but—it's a big price to pay."

"I know it, but it's worth all it will cost. Why I couldn't leave now, practically in the face of the enemy. I may not be a whole lot to the team, and probably there are fellows on the scrub who can play quarter-back as well, if not better, than I can. But I've trained with the boys all season. I'm their captain, however unworthy, and I've got to stick by 'em. It would be treason to go now. I've got to stick."

"But can't you do something? Can't you send Duncaster some word? He says he leaves to-night. Telegraph him that you'll see him directly after the game. Explain how things stand, and maybe he'll make allowances."

"I will," decided Dick, "but I haven't much hope. He is very much set against football, and he has no especial love for me. I can't understand why he should give in about the stock. Perhaps he feels that he must close up some of his business matters if he is going away. Then, too, dad's offer may be better than the one Porter made him. I can't understand it, but I'll take a chance and send him a wire, asking him to meet me after the game."

"Have you got the cash to pay for the stock?" asked Paul.

"Oh, I can give him a check to bind the bargain, and dad can settle with him later. I haven't as much in the bank as I had, for I let dad invest it in the electric line."

"Then you stand to lose too, if you don't get Duncaster's stock."

"Yes, but what of it? If we win this game, and Kentfield is the champion of the league, I'd be willing to lose almost all I had. I fancy dad left an offer with Mr. Duncaster, better than his first one, of an advance of ten per cent., and instructed the crabbed old chap to let him know when he was ready to accept it. Instead, he sends me word, and I—well, I'm not going—that's all. That is not until after the game. It's what dad would want me to do—he'll understand," said Dick softly.

"Well, you've got nerve—that's all I've got to say," complimented Paul admiringly.

Dick wrote his telegram, and he took the precaution to give Toots the money to prepay it.

"Duncaster might refuse it, if it went collect," he remarked with a grim smile. "I can't take any chances. Then, Toots, arrange to have a speedy taxicab waiting for me at the end of the game. I'll make a bee-line for Hardvale as soon as the last whistle blows," he explained to Paul. "Want to come along?"

"Sure."

It was almost time to go out on the gridiron now. Dick gave one brief and half-regretful thought to the opportunity he might be missing. Then he murmured:

"Well, the game—from now on!"

He had no idea of wiring his father the news, but he felt that after all it would be better to explain it personally.

"If dad was only where he could make a jump to Hardvale he could clinch the deal," he mused, "but it's impossible."

"Hark! What's that?" cried Paul as they were about to leave their room. It was the sound of a swelling, boisterous cry—a joyful shout—a challenge.

"The Blue team has arrived!" exclaimed Dick. "Come on! Now for the battle!"

Already there was quite a crowd in the grandstands, and more people were arriving every minute. The ticket takers had their hands full, and the ushers were as busy as bees. For rumors of the fierce game that was likely to be played had prevailed for the last two weeks, and there was every indication of a record-breaking crowd.

"Our treasury will be filled!" cried the manager of Kentfield with exultation. "This is a great day for us—even if we don't win."

"We're going to!" declared Dick with conviction.

As Dick turned around he saw a tall, well-formed young man approaching him. Something about the face seemed familiar, and, as the newcomer smiled, Dick remembered.

"Hello, Larry Dexter!" he exclaimed. "Where in the world did you blow from? Sent to report the game?"

"No, but I wish I was. I'm up here on a mystery case and, as I had a little time to spare I thought I'd see you fellows win. I heard about the game. Go in and beat!"

"Thanks! We're going to try. Say, but I am glad to see you, Larry. Come on over here and I'll see that you get a good seat. Or would you rather be on the side lines?"

"On the side lines I think." And Dick soon arranged so that his reporter friend would have a good place.

"See you later," he called as he went back on the field.

"I'm afraid not," answered Larry. "I'll have to get away in a hurry. I've got an appointment, but I'll stay long enough to see you pile up a good score," and though Dick looked for his friend after the game, he did not see him.

"Who is that?" asked Paul, as Dick joined him.

"That's Larry Dexter. One of the best reporters in New York. I met him when I was there, right after I got my fortune. He's a fine chap. But it's about time for the Blue Hill crowd to arrive."

Those of you who have read my Larry Dexter Series need no introduction to the hero of those books. Larry was a farm boy, who had an ambition to become a reporter on a big New York paper. In the book "From Office Boy to Reporter," I told how he did this, and in the other books of the series I related some of his strange adventures.

The Blue Hill cadets had come on a special train, and the team drove up from the station in a large carry-all that had been provided for them by Dick and his chums. A few days before the game the plans had been changed so as to bring the contest to Kentfield instead of having it on the Blue Hill gridiron.

"Well, you're on time, I see," said our hero, as he shook hands with Captain Haskell of Blue Hill. Haskell had been newly elected, to take the place of a friend who had unexpectedly been called away.

"Yes, and we're got our winning suits on."

"Well, we'll see about that," responded Dick with a quiet smile. "Now if you'll step over here we can arrange the details, and then both sides can have some practice."

"Sure," and a little later with the two coaches representing Kentfield, and two from Blue Hill, the captains conferred.

"I presume Blake will be all right for umpire," said Mr. Norton one of the visiting coaches.

"You mean George Blake—who umpired in our last game?" asked Mr. Spencer quickly.

"That's the one."

"We'd prefer some one else," said Mr. Spencer quietly, before Dick could interpose the objection that was on his lips.

"You don't like him? Why?" asked Captain Haskell quickly, with some wrath.

"Because he doesn't see all that goes on in the line," was the calm answer of the Princeton coach. "I don't believe it is necessary to say more."

"Well, if I——"

"It's all right," broke in Coach Norton for Blue Hill. "If you object to him, we'll take some one else. How will Jacob Small do?"

"Of Lehigh?"

"Yes."

"We'll accept him gladly," assented Mr. Spencer. "Now as to the other officials," and they were quickly settled upon.

"Heads or tails?" asked Dick, as he prepared to spin the coin for choice of goals.

"Um—heads," spoke Captain Haskell quickly, as the quarter went spinning into the air.

"Heads it is," announced Dick without a tremor in his voice. The first little indication of fate had gone against him, but it could not be helped. He hoped to get the choice, as there was no wind blowing, and naturally no advantage in goals, so that the winner of the toss could elect to have the other side kick off if he liked. Dick had planned to let Blue Hill kick if he had won the say of the spinning coin, but it was not to be. Which would Haskell select?

There was a moment's hesitation as the rival captain tested the wind with a moistened, up-lifted finger. Then he announced his choice.

"We'll take the north goal. You fellows can kick off!"

"All right," spoke Dick and he tried not to show the little disappointment in his voice. "Then as it's all settled we can get to practice."

Dick had hoped to get possession of the ball immediately after the kick off and by a series of whirlwind rushes demoralize his opponents. Now he would have to change his plans.

"Well, we'll see how we can hold them," he said to Paul, as they went over to their side of the field to run through some plays.

There was fast, snappy, preliminary work. Dick paused once or twice to observe his opponents.

"No sign of them going stale," he reflected.

The hour for play had come. The officials had settled all the details. The new ball had been blown up, and the cover laced tightly. Carrying it in his hand the referee advanced to the centre of the field and handed it to Dick.

"Are you ready?" the official asked.

The young millionaire nodded.

"Line up!" called the referee as Dick handed the ball to Innis Beeby to kick off.

CHAPTER XXIX

HAMMER AND SMASH

With a graceful curve the pigskin sailed down the field, high over the heads of the eager, waiting Blue Hill lads, beyond even their full-back who had not stationed himself far enough in the rear. He had to do a nimble sprinting act before he was ready to receive the spheroid on his ten yard line. Then, tucking the leather close to his chest, and with head well down he ran low back toward the Kentfield goal.

"Get to him, boy, get to him!" cried Dick. "We mustn't let 'em gain an inch if we can help it."

Like hounds from the leash, the young millionaire and his companions raced toward their quarry, and an instant later the two eager advancing lines met, eleven straining lads trying to bore in through ten others and get at the man with the ball.

Frank Rutley got him—it was Tod Kester, the big centre and Tod went down, a young mountain of flesh piling on top of him and the plucky left tackle. Now the real battle was about to begin, and the engagement was not long in opening.

"All ready. Kansas City—four hundred—six—eleven—twenty-six!"

Thus the sharp tones of Joe Bell the Blue Hill quarter, as he signalled his men. Then came a rush and there was a terrific impact on that part of the Kentfield line guarded by Paul Drew and Frank Rutley. It was a strain, but they stood it, and the wave of struggling humanity, in the centre of which was the Blue Hill left-half with the ball, was dashed back.

"No gain! That's good!" muttered Dick. "We're holding 'em!"

Again came the signal, and once more that terrific impact, but this time on the other side tackle and guard. Evidently Blue Hill was trying to find the weak spots.

Still again did Kentfield withstand it, and tossed back into their own territory their aggressive enemies.

"Watch out for a fake kick," Dick warned his chums, and they closed in—all but Hal Foster the full-back, who would not be drawn in to his disadvantage.

There was a quick signal, and a forward pass was tried. It came at a time when Dick and his chums were expecting either a kick or a fake kick, and showed what chances Blue Hill was willing to take. But they made good, for they gained several yards, and had the ball this much nearer Kentfield's goal. Dick felt a little sinking feeling at his heart, but he smiled bravely.

"We'll stop 'em next time," he said grimly.

Hammering and smashing again became the order of play, and at Kentfield's line came the Blue Hill lads with bulldog tenacity. But they had no weaklings to meet, and after a try through Drew and Rutley again, they endeavored to circle Weston's end. But the former crony of Porter was on the alert and like a snake he wiggled through the protecting interference and got his man when only one yard had been gained. Then to give his men a breathing spell Captain Haskell called for a kick, the ball being punted to Kentfield's fifteen yard line. Tom Colcton ran it back five yards before he was downed by a fierce tackle from Ned Buchanan, and then Dick and his mates had a chance to show what they could do.

"Smash 'em! Smash 'em!" murmured Paul in memory of his former game.

"Everybody keep cool," counseled Dick. "We don't want any penalties. Play a clean game. Get ready now."

In snapping tones he called the signal. It indicated that some sequence plays were to be tried—plays for which no further intimation would be given.

Between left tackle and guard plunged Ray Dutton, and before he could be stopped he had planted the ball five yards in advance toward Blue Hill's goal.

Another line up, and Hal Foster came plunging through a big hole that had been torn for him between centre and right guard. On and on he came, wiggling and squirming to gain every inch. In vain did Captain Haskell call on his men to stop the play. Kentfield seemed irresistible, and eight yards were reeled off, the grandstand contingent of our friends going wild with delight.

But Dick and his mates paid little attention to this. They had other matters to occupy them. There was another play to be made.

In silence, broken only by their panting breaths, the cadets again lined up, and as Jim Watkins passed the ball back to Dick, the latter shoved it into the waiting arms of John Stiver. John was on the run and with the aid of Rutley he sprang eagerly into the hole between the opposing left tackle and end, being preceded by Dutton who saw that the way was clear. It was a smashing attack, delivered at the right moment, Tom Coleton following in to see that no fumble was made. But none was, and ten clean yards were ripped off, a bigger gain than Blue Hill had yet made.

"Now, again, boys!" yelled Dick in delight, and now he gave the signal for an end run, that his panting lads might have some relief. It was Dutton's cue to take the ball around to the Blue Hill right end. But this was not so successful, as several of the opposing players were on the alert and were ready to nail him. He ran to one side and was actually forced back a yard before he went down.

"It might be worse," said Dick cheerfully. "We'll try it differently this time."

An on-side kick netted a good gain, and then came a forward pass, which was not so successful. There was a fumble—just whose fault it was could not be said—and one of the Blue Hill players fell on the ball while wild yells from their supporters told of the joy in their camp.

"Watch out now!" warned Dick again. But there was no kicking or trick play. Blue Hill was evidently going to depend on her slightly superior weight, and retain her line-smashing tactics. At Kentfield she came with a rush that carried her opponents off their feet for the time.

"Hold! Hold!" yelled Dick desperately, and his men tried to do so.

"Go on! Go on!" screamed Haskell. "Smash 'em to bits, but get through!"

Dick was watching for any slugging, but his opponents seemed to be playing a clean game. On came the man with the ball, and twelve yards had been ripped out through the very centre of the line of our heroes before they managed to nail Tom Hughes, who was worming his way forward with the pigskin.

So terrific was the next impact that Paul Drew went down and out and a pail of water was hastily called for. He was well soaked and massaged, until his breath came back with a gasp.

"Can you stay in?" asked Dick anxiously.

"Sure!" panted Paul, but his voice was not as strong as his captain would liked to have heard it.

"Stand by him," whispered the young millionaire to Frank Rutley. "They may try to put him out again."

Full two minutes were taken out to enable Paul to feel more like himself, and Dick was not mistaken when the next play was made. It was a terrific attack at Paul's place in the line. But sturdy Frank Rutley was ready for them, and John Stiver was also on the alert, so that when the Blue Hill's right half came plunging forward this time, he was met with such opposition that he reeled back gasping.

"Don't try here again!" called Frank to him significantly, and Paul breathed a bit easier. He was rapidly regaining his strength.

But though the attack had thus been hurled back once, the next time was not so successful and through a wide gap came the man with the ball with such fierceness and speed, that he reeled off fourteen yards, and now the pigskin was on Kentfield's thirty yard line.

"Look out for a try for goal," warned the captain, for he heard reports that Blue Hill had been practicing that for the past week, putting in a new man who had great abilities in the kicking line.

But the kick did not come, though the visitors made a fake attempt. It was only partially successful, however, and there was a fumble which enabled Dick to slip in and get the ball on a bounce. He was in two minds about what to do, but having sized up the mode of his opponents' playing, and reckoning the time left in the half, he decided to punt the ball back instead of keeping it and trying to advance it by rushing tactics.

"That will tire them if they want to begin smashing at our line again," he reasoned, "and will let Paul have a little more time. We're holding them all right, and maybe we can tire them more than they will us."

Thus in a flash he outlined his policy and sent the leather hurling back over the heads of the half-maddened Blue Hill lads who were chagrined at their fumbling.

"Come on!" cried the captain of the Kentfield lads. "We want to down their man in his tracks if we can."

It was almost done, and in fact the runner only managed to gain a few yards before he was fiercely thrown by Innis Beeby.

Again came that seemingly wearying, and never-ceasing attack on the line. But Dick's men were on the alert, and though another attempt was made through Paul he held firmly.

The pace was beginning to tell though, and panting breaths and palpitating hearts murmured their story. Dick resolved on more kicking if he got a chance at the ball. But it seemed that he was not to get it—at least right away. Once more up the field it was being advanced by short sharp rushes. Blue Hill seemed content to keep on with her bulldog playing, perhaps trusting that her men would last longer than would Dick's.

There was no denying the strength of the opponents of Kentfield. They were trained to the second, and the two coaches whom Dick's money had secured began to be a little direful of the result.

"Can they stand it?" asked Mr. Spencer of his colleague.

"Well, if they don't they're not what I think them to be," was the convincing answer.

The cheers and songs of the Blue Hill contingent seemed to give them added strength. They still had the ball, in spite of all the efforts of Dick and his men to hold them, to force a kick, or to get through and block the plays. Steadily and surely the leather was nearing the fatal line.

"Look out boys! Look out!" warned Dick. "Play hard."

He himself was working like a Trojan, getting into every opening, taking all kinds of hard knocks, really doing more than his share. Nor were there any shirkers in all the eleven. Hal Foster, at full, instead of staying back to be on the watch for kicks, or to block men who got through his mates, played well in. There was need of it, for Kentfield was being shoved back, and every ounce of weight to back her up told.

"Hold boys, hold!" begged and pleaded Dick desperately. He saw his goal line being menaced and it seemed as if Blue Hill, as she came nearer striking distance, grew wild with desire to cross it.

The fatal play came with such suddenness that it almost took the heart from Dick's cadets. After a smash at centre, which was hurled back, and a try between left tackle and guard, which netted only a yard, there was a quick shift to one side on the part of the Blue Hill players.

An instant later Dick saw Rud Newton, the stocky left half-back burst through with the ball under his arm. Like a flash the young millionaire sprang to tackle him, but he was not quite heavy enough, and Rud broke away. Full-back Foster was now Dick's only hope, but to his dismay he saw that Hal had been drawn in, and was now hopelessly entangled in the mass of his own and the opposing players.

There was not a soul between Newton and the Kentfield goal, and toward it the left half was now sprinting with all his speed. Dick gave a gasp, sprang to his feet and was off after him like a flash. But Newton had too much of a start, and the best the captain could do was to vainly touch him with outstretched hand a yard from the goal line. In another second Newton was over and had touched down the ball.

The first score had been made against Kentfield and the heart of Dick was sore as he slackened his pace and watched his own men and those of Blue Hill running up to witness the first act of the drama that meant so much to all of them.

CHAPTER XXX

THE WINNING TOUCHDOWN

Wild cries of delight, victorious shouts, the shrill voices of the girls, mingling with the hoarser tones of the men and youths, the waving of flags and banners, the shaking of canes adorned with the Blue Hill colors, showed the appreciation of the first gain in the battle.

"Yah! I thought your team was such a much!" yelled an ardent Blue Hill supporter to some Kentfield cadets in the stand next to him.

"So it is," was the cool answer, though there was a sore heart back of it. "We never play our best until the other team gets a touchdown. That's the only look-in your fellows will have."

"Oh, it is; eh?" demanded the other with a hoarse laugh. "Well, just watch our boys rip you all to pieces from now on."

The goal was kicked, making the score six to nothing against our friends, and Dick saw dubious looks on the faces of his chums.

"This is nothing!" he cried gaily. "It's the only taste of the honey-pot that we'll let them have. Come on now, we've got time to make a touchdown this half."

Play was resumed after the kick-off, and an exchange of punts followed, both sides seeming willing to take this method of regaining their strength, which had been almost played out.

When Blue Hill got the ball after a series of brilliant kicks that had delighted the spectators, she once more began her rushing tactics. But either some of her men were careless, or they were too eager, for they got off side, and there was some slugging which the alert umpire saw, and as a penalty the ball went to Dick's side.

"Now rush it up," he called eagerly, and then began such a whirlwind attack that Blue Hill was fairly carried off her feet. Right up the field from her own thirty-five yard line did Dick's men carry the pigskin, until on Blue Hill's twenty yard mark the young millionaire decided for a try for a field goal. It was a magnificent attempt but failed, and before any more playing could be started the whistle blew, ending the half.

Rather dejectedly Dick and his team filed to the dressing rooms. The two coaches met them.

"It's all right! It's all right!" cried Mr. Spencer. "You boys couldn't do better. You haven't made any mistakes. Keep on the same way next half and you'll have them."

"I hope so," murmured Dick.

"I know it!" declared Mr. Martin with conviction. "They can't keep up their pace, and they haven't any good subs to put in."

"That's right," agreed his colleague. "The way you carried the ball up the field after their touchdown showed what you could do. If there had been time you'd have scored. They can't stand that smashing attacking business, but you can hold them if you try. Then, at the right time, get the ball and take it up. One touchdown and goal will tie the score, and another touchdown will win the championship for you."

"Boys, will we do it?" cried Dick, turning to his cadets as they surrounded him in the dressing rooms under the grandstand.

"Will we?" cried Innis Beeby. "Will a duck eat corn meal, boys?"

"Sure!" came the enthusiastic answer.

Back again on the gridiron trotted the twenty-two sturdy lads to indulge in a little limbering-up practice before the second half should start. Then came the warning whistle.

"They'll kick off this time," said Dick to his men, "and that will give us the ball. We want to rush it right up the field without giving 'em time to catch their breaths. Try the sequence plays again, they worked well."

With a resounding "pung" the leather sailed into Kentfield territory. Beeby caught it and began a rush back that was not destined to last long, for with great fierceness he was tackled by Lem Gordon, and heavily thrown. But Beeby was as hard as nails, and arose smiling, keeping his foot on the ball.

"Now boys, play like mustard," called Dick, as a signal for the sequence plays, none other being given. The successive rushes that followed fairly carried the Blue Hill players off their feet, and so impetuously did Dick and his men smash into the line, going through centre, between guards and tackles, and around the ends that, inside of five minutes of play, the ball was on Blue Hill's ten yard line.

"Wow! Wow! Wow!" yelled enthusiastic Kentfield "rooters," and from being glum they were now wild with delight and eagerness.

"Touchdown! Touchdown!" came the imperative demand.

"Hold! Hold 'em!" pleaded the Blue Hill throng.

"They ought to make it now or never," said a gray-haired man as he half rose to watch the next play. "They must shove it over if they work as they have all the way up the field."

Dick paused for a moment. He was deciding on the next play. Blue Hill was frantic and might take any unfair advantage. The Kentfield men were like hounds after a stag—it seemed that nothing could keep them back. Dick sent Ray Dutton through centre for five yards.

He came back into the line gasping, for he had been tackled hard.

"Only a little more now, fellows!" yelled the captain. "Nothing can stop us now."

"Yes, we can!" cried Haskell in desperation. "Don't let 'em through, boys!"

His half-wild players managed to stop Stiver with the ball after a three yard gain. But two more yards were needed—six feet.

Dick gave the signal for big Beeby to take the ball, and the next instant the sturdy guard had hurled himself into the gap made for him. For a second or two it seemed that he could not make it, so fiercely did Blue Hill brace. Then, slowly but surely they began giving way under the terrific pressure of the eager Kentfield cadets, and then came a wild yell from Beeby, who was half smothered under a mass of players.

"Down!" he gasped, and with his last strength cried "Touchdown!"

The heap of players slowly dissolved. For a moment the spectators were in doubt, and then, as the meaning of the joyous dancing about of Kentfield, and the glum appearance of her opponents was borne to them, the sympathizers of Dick's team burst into a frenzy of shouts and cheers while the flags and banners were riotously waved in the maze of color.

The score was tied a moment later as the goal was kicked. Who would make the next points?

Quickly the ball was put into play again, and there followed an exchange of punts—a grateful relief from the line-smashing tactics that had carried the pigskin over the goal mark. It was a rest for both sides for Blue Hill had been played almost to a standstill and Dick's men were panting and gasping from their terrific efforts. But it seemed worth all it cost.

Seldom had there been such a situation in the annals of the Military League. Two of the best teams that had ever been represented playing such fast football, and the score tied at such a critical moment meant something. Add to it that the elevens were not on the most friendly feeling, because of what had taken place early in the season, and there was a situation that would make even a blasé football enthusiast "sit up and take notice," as Innis Beeby said.

The slightest turn of events might send the scale up or down now, bringing victory or defeat. For a time both sides played warily, taking no chances for the championship hung on the next few minutes.

Then, as Dick's side got the spheroid, he called for some more of the terrific playing. Nobly his men responded and eagerly. Almost too eagerly it seemed for there was a fumble at a critical point and one of the Blue Hill men seized the ball. Back toward the Kentfield goal he sprinted with it, and for a moment Dick nearly had "heart disease" as he said afterward. But this time Teddy Naylor, who had gone in to replace Hal Foster at full, because Hal's weak ankle went back on him, tackled the man, and the danger was over. But Blue Hill had the ball, and took advantage of it by kicking it far enough away so that Kentfield would have to work hard to regain the lost ground.

"Smash 'em! Smash 'em!" ordered Dick, as his men lined up. So fierce was the attack and the offense that Paul Drew was knocked out, and could not come back in time to play. Ford Baker went in.

This was rather a blow to Dick, and when John Stiver keeled over a little later, from a blow on the head, the chances of Kentfield were not improved. Sam Wilson went in at left half, and his playing was a distinct revelation, for he jumped into the line with such energy that he tore off ten yards on his first play.

"Good!" cried Dick. "A few more like that and we'll have the game."

The half was nearing a close. There had been more kicking, and several scrimmages. Then Blue Hill had the ball, and Haskell called on his cadets for a last desperate effort. They responded nobly, and Dick's team, weakened as they were by the extraordinary hard pace, began to give way.

Up the field they were shoved until they made a stand on their twenty yard line.

"We've got to hold if we want the championship," said Dick simply, but his words meant much.

And then came one of the surprises of football. The people on the stands were holding their breaths in anxiety, each individual almost praying for his particular team. It looked bad for Kentfield, as she was being steadily shoved back, and the time was fast passing. It seemed that she would either be beaten, or that a tie game would result, necessitating another conflict.

Haskell gave orders for a fake kick, and so often had he worked that play during the game that Dick's men at once were aware of what was going to happen. Around the end of the line came smashing the Blue Hill full-back who had taken the ball from his left half-back. Right around he came, but Dick was there to tackle him. With all the fierceness and energy of which he was capable the young millionaire sprang at his man. They came down together.

The ball rolled from the full-back's arms at his impact with the earth, and like a flash Dick saw his chance. He was up in an instant, had grabbed the leather, tucked it under his arm and was racing down the field toward the goal of his enemies.

He had a ninety yard run ahead of him, and the Blue Hill full back was waiting for him with open arms. How he got past Dick never knew, but those watching saw him fiercely bowl over his opponent like a tenpin. Then on and on he sprinted, while a wild riot of yells from the grandstands urged him forward.

On and on he ran—on and on. His breath was rasping through his clenched teeth— his legs seemed like sticks of wood, that were somehow actuated by springs which were fast losing their power.

"Can I do it?" he gasped. Then he answered himself. "I'm *going to do it*!"

He heard the pounding of feet behind him, but he dared not look back. On he kept. Chalk mark after chalk mark passed beneath his vision. At last he ceased to see them. He looked for the goal posts. They seemed miles away, but were gradually coming nearer through a mist.

He felt someone touch him from behind. He heard the panting breath of a runner—he felt his jacket scraped by eager fingers, but he kept on.

Then, when he had no more breath left; when it was all black before his eyes, he crossed the last line—fairly staggered over it and fell with the ball in the final touchdown—the score that won the game—for the whistle blew as his men and their enemies were running up.

Dick had won the championship.

CHAPTER XXXI

THE TROLLEY STOCK—CONCLUSION

The grandstands were trembling and swaying under the foot-stamping, yelling crowd that enthusiastically cheered the victorious Kentfield cadets. Dick felt as if it was all a dream until he found himself half lifted to his feet and felt his comrades clapping him on the back, yelling congratulations in his ears, while a dozen or more were trying to shake his hand at once, for the gridiron had been overwhelmed by a riotous throng of substitutes and spectators as soon as the final whistle blew.

"Oh, Dick! Dick!" cried Paul, limping up to his chum.

"We—we did 'em!" gasped the captain.

"*We* did 'em?" questioned Dutton, also among the cripples. "*You* did 'em you mean, Dick Hamilton. It's your team from start to finish!"

"Oh, bosh!" cried our hero.

There was a lull in the cheering on the stands, and suddenly, in the silence, there broke out the shrill voice of an old man—evidently one unused to football games.

"By heck!" he cried, "That was a great run! I never see a better one! Golly, but he scooted. This is the first time I ever see one of these games, but it won't be the last! Who was it made that home run."

So still was it that Dick could hear the question and answer for he was not far from the stand.

"It wasn't a home run," some one informed the old man, "it was a run for a touchdown, and Dick Hamilton, the Kentfield captain, made it."

"Dick Hamilton? Where is he now? I want to see him. I've got something to say to him."

As in a dream Dick wondered where he had heard that voice before. Then like a flash it came to him—Enos Duncaster! But Mr. Duncaster at a football game—one between teams of the "tin soldiers" whom he affected to despise. It seemed impossible. Dick looked to where the old man was now vigorously applauding though every one else was quiet. There could be no mistake. It *was* Mr. Duncaster—the holder of the trolley stock. Yet how came he at the game?

"I want to see him. I want to see that Dick Hamilton!" Mr. Duncaster was saying. "I came to see him—I've got important news for him, and I'm in a hurry."

"You'd better go to him, Dick," advised Paul. "Maybe it isn't too late about that stock."

Dick felt a thrill of hope. At intervals of the game he had half regretted his decision to play instead of going to keep the appointment with the eccentric rich man. He had feared it would be too late, and that his message to Mr. Duncaster would set that peculiar individual against him.

Dick turned his steps toward where Mr. Duncaster stood in the grandstand. As the youth passed along he was congratulated on all sides.

"Great run, Hamilton! Great!" was called again and again.

"I want to shake hands with you, Dick Hamilton!" exclaimed Mr. Duncaster heartily. "And I want to say I've got a different opinion of you boys than I had. I guess I was mistaken.

"Just after I sent you that message, saying your father could have the stock, I picked up a magazine and read an account of a football game. It was the first I'd ever read, and thinks I to myself I'd like to see it. Then, when I got your message saying you were going to play, and couldn't come to see me I made up my mind to come to see you. I did, and by heck! it was great—great! But your run was the best of all.

"First I was a little put out because you didn't come to see me, and I half made up my mind to give the stock to Mr. Porter. But I see now why you wanted to stay and play the game. You couldn't desert, and by heck! I'm glad you won! Shake hands again!"

Dick did so, in a mist of tears that would not be kept back. The reaction was almost too much for him. To win the championship, and in the next breath to be told that his father's plans need not fail, was almost too much.

He managed to stammer out his thanks to Enos Duncaster, whom many spectators were regarding curiously.

"You cadets are all right!" the old man was saying. "It takes more spunk than I imagined to smash into each other that way. I'm coming to all the football games after this—that is as soon as I get my health back. I'm off for Europe now. I've just about got time to catch my train.

"Here's the stock your father wants, Dick Hamilton. I've got it all ready for you in a bundle, and inside is the address of my lawyers. You can——"

"But the pay——" stammered Dick.

"That's all right—you can send it to my lawyers. I'm in a hurry. Now good-bye—I'm off to the hot springs!" And once more he wrung Dick's hand. "That was a great run—great!" cried Mr. Duncaster, as he made his way off the stand.

"Three cheers for Dick Hamilton!" called Ray Dutton.

And how the people did cheer!

"And three for Mr. Duncaster—a convert to football!" shouted Paul Drew, and if they were not as loud as the first cheers they must have warmed the old man's heart.

Dick sent a telegram to his father conveying double good news—about the football victory and about the possession of the stock.

"I guess your troubles will be over now dad," wired Dick.

They were seemingly for a time, but later other financial matters involved Dick and his father, and how they turned out, and how Dick met them will be told in the next volume of this series, to be called "Dick Hamilton's Touring Car; Or, A Young Millionaire's Race for a Fortune." In it we shall meet Dick and his friends and some of his enemies, and learn how he triumphed over the latter.

There was great rejoicing in Kentfield that night when the team broke training and the suits were burned. True to his word, Dick provided the finest banquet the cadets had ever had spread in their honor. There were speeches innumerable, and the coaches were given their full share of praise.

But it was toward Dick that most eyes were turned and he was called on again and again to respond to a toast.

"Well, which do you feel better over, Dick?" asked Paul that night, as they went to their room, "winning the championship or getting the stock from Mr. Duncaster?"

"Both," replied the young millionaire with a smile. "But it certainly was great to convert Mr. Duncaster into a gridiron rooter; eh, Grit?"

And Grit whined in delight, jumping up on Dick, while the two chums sat down in the little room and played the great game all over again.

End of the book.

www.ingramcontent.com/pod-product-compliance
Lightning Source LLC
Chambersburg PA
CBHW070649290526
45790CB00001B/236